FEB 2 2 1999

S0-BSG-840

PROPERTY
OF THE
FARGO PUBLIC LIBRARY

AN INTRODUCTION TO

ILLUSTRATION

AN INTRODUCTION TO
ILLUSTRATION

BRIAN LEWIS

Grange
BOOKS

A QUINTET BOOK

Published by Grange Books
An Imprint of Grange Books plc
The Grange
Grange Yard
London SE1 3AG

This edition published 1995

ISBN 1-85627-895-6

Copyright © 1987 Quintet Publishing Limited.
All rights reserved. No part of this publication
may be reproduced, stored in a retrieval system
or transmitted in any form or by any means,
electronic, mechanical, photocopying, recording
or otherwise, without the permission of the
copyright holder.

This book was designed and produced by
Quintet Publishing Limited
6 Blundell Street
London N7 9BH

Creative Director: Peter Bridgewater
Editor: Hazel Harrison

Typeset in Great Britain by
Central Southern Typesetters, Eastbourne
Manufactured in Hong Kong by
Regent Publishing Services Limited
Printed in Singapore by
Star Standard Industries (Pte) Ltd

The author would like to thank all the artists who
gave so generously of their time in discussing their
work. Special thanks to Christine Isteed of Artist
Partners Ltd without whose help this book would
still be an idea at the end of the telephone line.

O
741.2
L613
c.1

CONTENTS

FOREWORD

This book is aimed at both the student and the interested amateur who would like to gain some knowledge of the processes available to the illustrator.

It is divided into three sections, the first dealing with the materials and methods for immediate image-producing, such as pencil and paint; the second describing the methods of making prints; and the third showing a *selection* of work from *some* of the many areas for which illustrative work is required. The third section indicates the technical process in each case, but pays particular attention to the working response to a specific brief or commission. Where possible I have indicated the client's instructions, and have shown the stages of the illustrator's work that demonstrate the ability to adapt in response to a particular brief. It must be emphasized that the work shown here is only a fraction, and a focused fraction at that, of the very diverse images that constitute illustration.

Illustrators are usually asked to work larger than the intended reproduction size, and their work is then reduced to the required measure. The format of this book has frequently entailed dramatic reductions in scale, but sections of some work have been reproduced "same size", in order to indicate the technique.

In the first two sections of the book the divisions come naturally, following the order of the obvious types of image production. Some of these happen to be popular at the moment, while others, although not used extensively today, have a significant place in the history of illustration, and may easily emerge again as fashionable techniques. There is one important category that lacks its own heading. This is "mixed media", and in this case I have chosen to deal with such mixtures of material and technique where they fit easily into the discussion of a particular medium. It is part of the illustrator's manner of working to mix and adapt media in order to solve a particular problem.

Wherever possible I have illustrated the discussion of each medium with the work of contemporary illustrators, and these images, together with the accompanying text, provide specific insights into the use of methods and materials. Some illustration practices are highly individual to a particular artist, but inventiveness is the hallmark of a good illustrator, and most artists will develop their own "tricks", either by happy accident or in desperation born of time pressures.

I would like to close this foreword with one of the many anecdotes that have come my way in the course of putting together this book. An illustrator working under pressure of a deadline had cleaned his brushes in washing-up liquid after completing a passage. He resumed work on the image and began to apply the acrylic paint with his newly-cleaned brushes, which still retained some of the detergent in their bristles. Bubbles appeared in the paint layer. Instead of panicking, however, the artist let the work dry, and found he had created an effect of random and varied circles in the colour. This "technique" has been part of his illustrative armoury ever since.

*I*NTRODUCTION

Illumination depicting St Matthew from the early 9th-century *Book of Kells.*

Above Illumination from St John's Manuscript
(11th century).

Right Illustration depicting three cats from a 13th-
century bestiary.

In order to put the images in this book into context it will be helpful to define the word "illustration" and to consider exactly what it means.

We can perhaps start with the assumption that illustrations are images associated with words, which means that we can rule out message-bearing images, such as cave paintings and religious mosaics. A good starting point is medieval manuscript books, and one important aspect of illustration is the skilful use of two-dimensional design as opposed to spatial, painterly images which attempt to convey the third dimension. The capacity to explore the world of flat pattern in a creative way is clearly shown in the early 9th-century illuminated manuscript *The Book of Kells*, with its marvellous swirling design displaying a fascination with interlacing pattern based on letter forms.

The medieval illustrated books were special productions for ceremonial occasions and display, and the artist was often called upon not merely to decorate but to elucidate the text – that is, to produce images that had a practical function. The immediate concern was the usually symbolic visual content; the everyday appearance of a person or object was not important. Thus, in the late 7th- or early 8th-century *Lindisfarne Gospels*, the gestures of the figures are rather overstated and the surrounding environment is reduced to a stage-set appearance, providing an early example of the virtues of clarity and economy of style.

These illustrations were very important as an aid to comprehension in an age of very limited literacy. The scribe wrote the text while the painter provided the miniatures, created initials and decorated borders. It is often thought that all this work took place in monasteries, but in fact this is not so; some of the practitioners were secular and, at least by the 12th century, so were many of the clients. Increasing secularization brought, in time, new interest in naturalism and the depiction of contemporary life, complete with details of architecture and dress. Sometimes illustrations covered a whole page, particularly in the case of the "books of hours" (prayer books for the laity). In the 15th century the great innovators in naturalism were the Limbourg Brothers, whose most notable work was the *Très Riches Heures du Duc de Berri*.

Sometimes the images were almost more important than the words – for example, in the sometimes fanciful herbals and bestiaries, in which the pictures were purely descriptive, or at least meant to be. Leonardo da Vinci, in his scientific notebooks, considered it to be the task of the words to explain the image, and pictures whose purpose is the communication of information have a significant place in the story of illustration.

Technical and commercial developments in the 19th century had a marked effect on both the volume and the nature of illustration. The mass production of newspapers and magazines opened up the new areas: manufacturers and tradesmen needed images, both for the press and for posters, and once the advantages of attractive packaging had been appreciated, another field evolved for the commercial artist.

The development of photography had a considerable impact on the illustrator and his or her images, and photomechanical printing methods freed the designer from the restrictions of the traditional printing processes, allowing a greater range of media to be used for producing artwork. The photographic image itself affected the nature of the product, with some artists using it directly in collages, some copying it in order to obtain a sharp realism, and others amplifying and reinforcing its qualities in order to create the super-realism of, for example, the airbrush techniques. Yet others rejected it altogether and went their own way.

Three major threads in illustration in the present day, are the production of diverting decoration; the creation of imaginative or realistic elucidation of a text; the precise delineation of technical and scientific subjects which are described and explained on the printed page.

Although obviously there is some truth in the standard definition of illustration as "pictures that clarify an idea or text", the concept of illustration as "images that serve a purpose" seems to be even more relevant to the vast range of modern-day work.

EQUIPMENT AND MATERIALS

CHARCOAL AND PENCILS

The choice of equipment and materials depends very much on the job in hand and the chosen area of the artist's work. Here is a selection of items used by artists generally and illustrators in particular.

Below Popular types of colour pencils are Derwent **1**, thin lead colour pencils **2** and Caran d'Ache **3**. Also Derwent colour blocks **4**, Blackedge **5** which is a type of layout pencil, col-erase **6** a completely erasable colour pencil, All-Stabilos **7** and chinagraphs **8**.

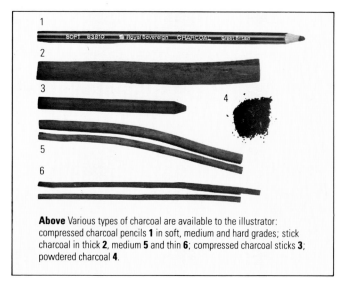

Above Various types of charcoal are available to the illustrator: compressed charcoal pencils **1** in soft, medium and hard grades; stick charcoal in thick **2**, medium **5** and thin **6**; compressed charcoal sticks **3**; powdered charcoal **4**.

Above The wood-encased graphite pencil, the clutch pencil and the propelling pencil are the three main types used in drawing.

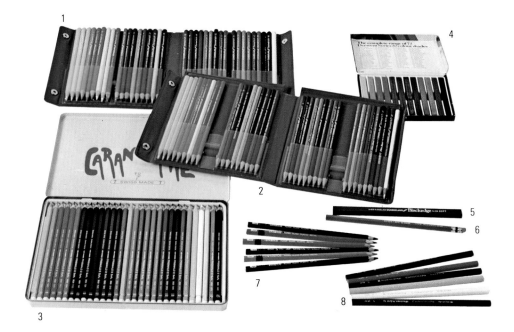

Below Graphite pencils are usually available in a range from 8H (very hard) to 8B (very soft), with H and B being the least hard and soft of their respective groups. In the middle of the range are F and HB, with F being slightly harder than HB.

PASTELS AND PENS

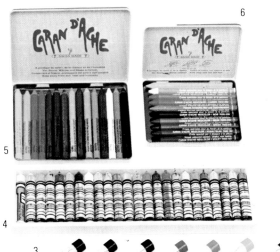

Left Pastels, chalks and crayons are available in various ranges. Some makes of soft pastels **1** are available in a wide variety of tints, from 0 (light) to 8 (dark). Pastel pencils **2** are lightproof and non-toxic. Wax crayons **3** are non-toxic, light- and water-resistant. Oil pastels **4** can be blended on the paper and do not need fixing. Caran d'Ache produce ordinary crayons in two ranges, hard to medium **5** and soft **6**, Conté crayons **7** are similar to natural chalks, but their colour range is limited.

Below The technical pen **1** produces a regular, even line by means of tubular nibs which are available in a variety of widths. The Graphos reservoir pen **2** takes a variety of nib types. Although rather outdated the traditional dip pen **3** is still popular.

Above Marker pens are becoming increasingly popular with illustrators. Felt-tip markers **5** provide a broader line and are available in a wide range of colours **1**. Fibre-tip markers range from fine **2** to medium **3, 4**.

Waterproof inks are also available in a wide range of colours **6, 7, 8** as well as the traditional black and white **9**.

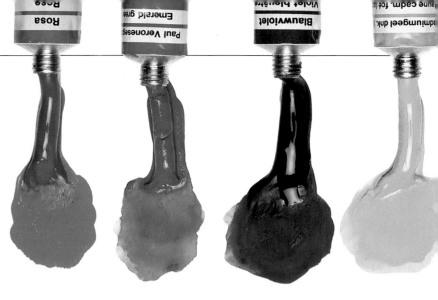

PIGMENT AND PAINT

ACRYLIC

Below right Acrylics are available in all the established colours as well as a considerable range of new, scientifically produced colours. Acrylic used straight from the tube gives a semi-matt finish, but it can also be heavily diluted and used like watercolour paint. Mix with acrylic media for thick impastos or textured finishes.

TEMPERA

Below and bottom Tempera paint is made by mixing powdered pigment with an egg solution. Pigments are available in a wide range of strong colours **bottom**, and ready-mixed tempera **below** can also be obtained, although in a more restricted palette.

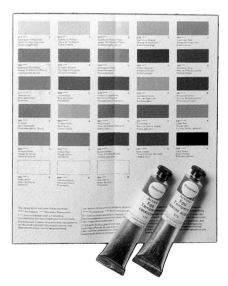

GOUACHE
Above Gouache, or 'designers' colour' is available in a wide range of colours in both tube and cake form. It is especially popular with illustrators because of its natural opacity, which reproduces well.

BLENDING BRUSH
A large blending brush is particularly useful for scumbling, applying texture and blending wet colours.

BRUSHES
For gouache, acrylic and tempera use the types of brushes usually associated with watercolour painting. **Far right** from top to bottom: sable lettering, sable round, sable bright, sable fan, pony/camel round, ox-hair round, squirrel round, mixed fibres round, synthetic round.

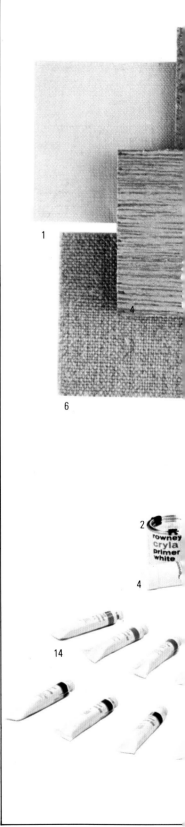

WATERCOLOUR PAINTS

Watercolour paints are available in a wide variety of forms. Bottled, concentrated watercolours **middle** are used when a particularly striking hue is required. Half pans **top and middle left** are particularly popular, and can be purchased separately or in sets. Boxed pans **left and right** are useful in that they can double as palettes. Tubes **bottom** are rather messy to use, as they have to be squeezed on to the palette before use.

OIL PAINTS & EQUIPMENT

Left The most commonly used support for oil paint is the traditional canvas (a stretched fabric support). Various fabrics can be used according to the tone and texture required, for example, white unprimed calico **1**, brown unprimed linen **6**, and primed hessian **3**. Ready-primed canvas can be purchased **8**, but tends to be expensive. Wood can also be used, but does tend to warp and split. Well-seasoned hardwoods, like mahogany **4**, are suitable if primed and braced, as are thick plywood **5** and hardboard **2**.

Below left An unprepared support must be protected with size **1** and ground to prevent the oil in the paint from effecting the support. Three types of ground are acrylic **2**, gesso **3** and emulsion **4**. Unprepared, ground pigment is mixed with a binder, either linseed oil **5, 7** or poppy oil **6, 8**. A medium, such as a mixture of turpentine **9** and linseed oil, makes it easier to apply the paint. Various materials are used for palettes, such as wood **10**, paper **12**, plastic **13** and metal **11**. Ready prepared oil colours **14** are available in a good range of colours.

Above right Good quality brushes, in a range of shapes, are essential. From **top to bottom**, ox-hair wide, blender, squirrel round, sable fan, sable flat, hogs-hair filbert, hogs-hair round, hogs-hair bright.

Above The three basic shapes of brush used in oil painting are from **left to right** bright, filbert and round.

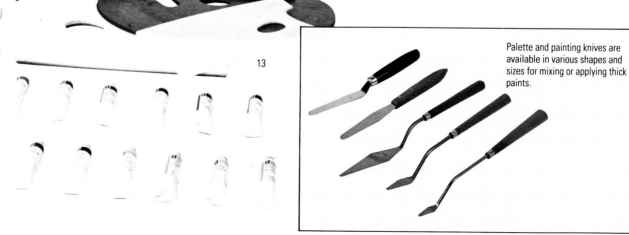

Palette and painting knives are available in various shapes and sizes for mixing or applying thick paints.

EASELS AND EQUIPMENT

WORK SURFACES
The choice of work surface varies from illustrator to illustrator, although a stable surface is the essential quality to look out for. The combination easel **1** is both a folding studio easel and a drawing table and ideal if studio space is limited. Basic drawing boards **below left** provide a basic smooth surface and can be purchased in a variety of sizes and materials, such as wood **2**, and formica covered for easy cleaning **3**. The adjustable model **4** has a drafting head that can be fixed in any position. Adjustable drawing boards **5, 6** for use on a table top will provide an angled surface, while the drawing stand **8** offers the same flexibility in a self-contained unit. The Rotoboard **7** can be used for work requiring multiple ruling.

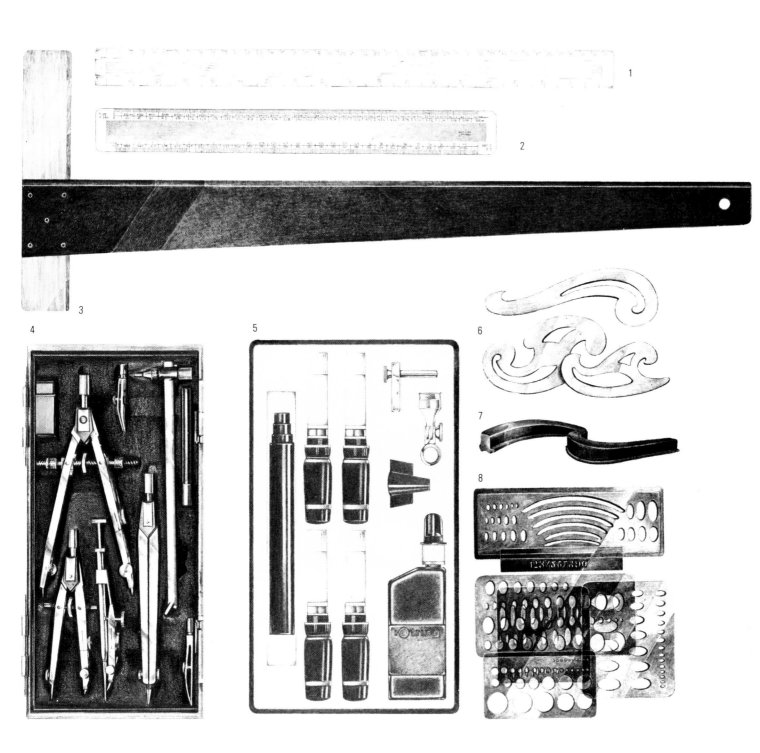

A standard ruler **1** is an essential piece of basic equipment, and a scale version **2** is particularly useful in technical drawing to enlarge or diminish the scale.

Various sizes of T-square **3** are available and are used in drawing accurate parallel lines.

A set of drawing instruments **4** is essential for technical drawing, and a basic set should include two sizes of spring bow compass, dividers, small radius compass, ruling pens and extension bar for drawing larger circles.

Technical drawing pens **5** are used by illustrators in all fields of work, and are not confined to purely technical drawing.

Drawing aids, such as French curves **6**, flexible curve **7** and templates **8** are required by the illustrator in the production of many types of image.

PAPER

Right Good art papers have a clearly defined watermark, which will indicate the right side of the paper to use. The three basic types of papers available are (from left to right) hot-pressed, with a smooth surface, cold-pressed or 'not', a medium texture, and rough, which has a coarse texture as its name implies. They are also available in a variety of weights (light, thin papers need stretching), and colours.

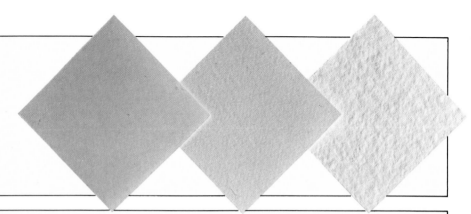

STUDIO EQUIPMENT

1 Spray adhesive
2 Rubber cement glue
3 Invisible mending tape
4 Clear adhesive tape
5 Double-sided tape
6 Drafting tape
7 Gummed brown tape
8 Stapler
9 Staple remover
10 Blades
11 Retractable craft knife
12 Craft knife
13 Scalpel
14 Stanley knife
15 Retractable craft knife
16 Flexicurve
17 Adjustable triangle
18 Metal rule
19 Plastic rule
20 Scissors
21 Translucent cutting mat
22 Cutting mat
23 French curves
24 Kneaded eraser
25 Vinyl eraser
26 Gum eraser
27 Ink eraser
28 Sandpaper blocks

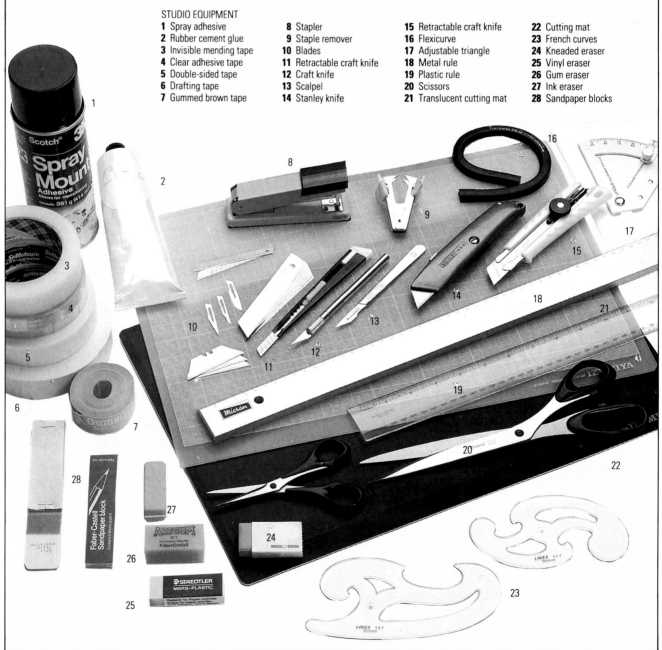

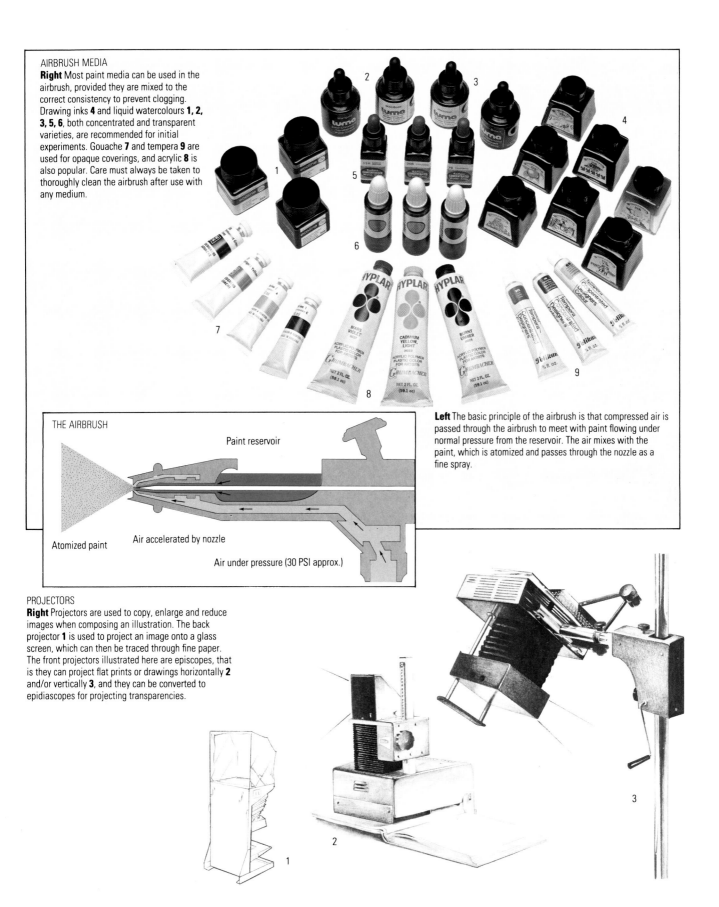

AIRBRUSH MEDIA

Right Most paint media can be used in the airbrush, provided they are mixed to the correct consistency to prevent clogging. Drawing inks **4** and liquid watercolours **1, 2, 3, 5, 6**, both concentrated and transparent varieties, are recommended for initial experiments. Gouache **7** and tempera **9** are used for opaque coverings, and acrylic **8** is also popular. Care must always be taken to thoroughly clean the airbrush after use with any medium.

THE AIRBRUSH

Paint reservoir

Atomized paint

Air accelerated by nozzle

Air under pressure (30 PSI approx.)

Left The basic principle of the airbrush is that compressed air is passed through the airbrush to meet with paint flowing under normal pressure from the reservoir. The air mixes with the paint, which is atomized and passes through the nozzle as a fine spray.

PROJECTORS

Right Projectors are used to copy, enlarge and reduce images when composing an illustration. The back projector **1** is used to project an image onto a glass screen, which can then be traced through fine paper. The front projectors illustrated here are episcopes, that is they can project flat prints or drawings horizontally **2** and/or vertically **3**, and they can be converted to epidiascopes for projecting transparencies.

PRINTING MATERIALS

LINOCUT

Above Linocut Special gouges that fit into an all-purpose handle are available for 'drawing' on linoleum. A rubber roller is used to apply ink to the surface of the linocut before printing.

LITHOGRAPHY

Right Lithography Litho crayons and chalks are available in various forms. The standard square crayon stick (middle) is a mixture of black pigment and grease. A cleaner form is available encased in wood and litho ink (bottom) must be melted and mixed with water.

WOOD BLOCKS

Top Wood blocks The end-grain block **above** is used for wood engraving, and a long grain block **bottom** for woodcut.

INTAGLIO ENGRAVING

Right Intaglio engraving Basic equipment should include a copper or zinc plate, a sandbag to support it while engraving, and two sharpened burins.

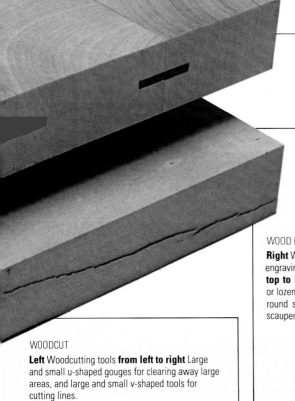

WOOD ENGRAVING

Right Wood engraving tools **from top to bottom** Gravure or lozenge, spitstick, round scauper, square scauper.

WOODCUT

Left Woodcutting tools **from left to right** Large and small u-shaped gouges for clearing away large areas, and large and small v-shaped tools for cutting lines.

INTAGLIO ETCHING

Below Intaglio etching materials The following materials are used in making an etching. A gas blow lamp **1** for heating the plate, and white chalk for cleaning **2**; stop-out varnish **3**; acid **4** for the etching process; granulated sugar **5**; a pestle and mortar **6** for pounding bitumen; a leather roller **7** for spreading ground; a measuring jar **8**; drawing ink **9**; ready prepared grounds **10**; an etching needle **11** for drawing; a brush or feather **12** for removing bubbles during etching; a metal clamp **13**; tapers **14** for blackening; metal plates **15**.

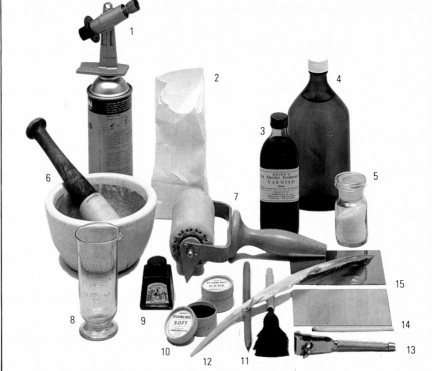

PENCIL, PAINT AND ALLIED MEDIA

CHARCOAL

Charcoal, which is carbonized wood, is the most basic of the single-point media. Carbonization is the production of a form of carbon by partially burning wood – most frequently willow or vine twigs – in the absence of air. Charcoal has had a humble but essential role in the history of art, and has been used universally as a medium for making sketches and studies, though more rarely for producing finished artwork. In the 19th century it was frequently used in combination with other media by such artists as the ever-inventive Edgar Degas (1834–1917) and Henri de Toulouse-Lautrec (1864–1901).

Stick charcoal is made in a variety of thicknesses and grades. The sticks are fragile, but can be sharpened with either a knife or sandpaper. Less fragile are charcoal crayons, which are made by pressing powdered charcoal into regular-sized crayon-like sticks, and charcoal pencils, which are thin sticks of compressed charcoal encased in wood. These are graded in the same way as graphite pencils, and are much cleaner to use than stick charcoal, as well as being easier to sharpen.

However, for a free-flowing style on a large scale, a stick of charcoal, whether sharpened to produce fine lines or used on its side to make broad even marks, is ideal. Areas of tone can be created by rubbing the charcoal marks with the fingers or with stumps of rolled paper called tortillons or torchons and a kneadable eraser (putty rubber) shaped into a point is invaluable for producing highlights in an area of tone. To avoid smudging a completed area should be fixed.

Below Albrecht Dürer *Portrait of a Young Man*. This portrait illustrates how charcoal can be used effectively for both line and tone drawing.

CHARCOAL TECHNIQUES

SPREADING CHARCOAL WITH A TORTILLON Lay the design and spread the charcoal with a tortillon over the surface of the paper **1** to create the subtle graduation of tone **2**.

CHARCOAL WITH A WASH **1** Draw a solid shape with the flat of the charcoal stick, and add radiating lines with the point. **2** Using a brush dipped in clean water, work over the design to soften the harshness of the black areas. Allow the wash to dry before adding more charcoal detail.

Above Colin Williams *Seated Figure:* charcoal, 31 × 38 in (79 × 96 cm)

Above Colin Williams *Tchaikovsky:* charcoal, 22 × 33 in (56 × 58 cm)

Seated Figure

The nature of charcoal and the kind of marks it makes encourages the artist to work on a large scale and very directly.

This is an example of an "immediate" use of the medium. No preliminary marks were made, and the artist began by launching into the areas that interested him most, the face and eyes in particular. The handling is quite aggressive, producing strong marks, and there is dramatic emphasis in the exaggeration of the hands. The approach is essentially linear, most of the tone being established using the side of the charcoal stick rather than by smudging. Dark areas were built up by first fixing a layer and then working into it, in some places with cross-hatching. Indian ink was used to sharpen the definition of the hands and mouth and again the charcoal was fixed beforehand.

Tchaikovsky

The client was interested in the artist's use of charcoal on cardboard and asked him to use that combination for a series of sheet-music covers. Cardboard provides a responsive surface for charcoal, and Colin Williams experiments with a wide variety of discarded pieces.

The image was worked out on tracing paper before being transferred to the cardboard. The subtle variations in the light tones were established by using layout paper, absorbent paper towels and watercolour paper glued down, and details were then re-established in charcoal on the collaged paper. Further tonal variation was achieved by crumpling paper and then ironing it out so that the creases were firmly defined, and Indian ink was painted on to intensify and define certain areas.

Two Into One Won't Go

A charcoal drawing showing both line and tones was established and then fixed, after which coloured crayons were used to indicate pattern and strong, vivid washes of watercolour were added. The texture of the watercolour paper reflects through the charcoal line giving a pleasing texture.

Above Nick Sharratt *Two into One Won't Go:* charcoal and watercolour, 12 × 11 in (30 × 28 cm)

PENCIL AND COLOURED PENCIL

The so-called "lead" of a pencil is actually not lead, but a mixture of graphite and clay; the more clay the softer the pencil. The process of mixing the two materials was invented by Nicholas-Jacques Conté (1755–1805) toward the end of the 18th century, and in the following century pencil became established as a medium for sketching, finished artwork and book illustration.

The grading of a pencil indicates the type of mark that will be made on the paper. Pencils can be purchased in a range from 8H, a very hard pencil acting like a stylus on the paper, to 8B, a very soft pencil which produces a chalk-like line. Within their respective categories, H is the least hard and B is the least soft. In the middle of the range are F and HB, both medium-grade pencils, with F being slightly harder than HB.

Pencil point can be used to make a variety of marks – from dots to graduated line – and within these marks considerable variations can be achieved by changes in pressure. Outline drawings are usually done with a fairly hard-leaded pencil, with tones most frequently built up by using softer pencils, either in a careful cross-hatching technique or smudged to give a smooth transition.

Many different types of paper can be used, from textured hand-made papers to brown wrapping paper, and their individual textures have an effect on the finished work. Pencil responds well to the surface quality of paper as long as it has some tooth; on a shiny surface the pencil will slip and make little or no mark.

Coloured pencils made a later appearance on the

Left J. A. D. Ingres *La Famille Stamaty* This study shows a rather stark linear approach, with little use of shading.

scene. They were developed in the late 19th century, and are made from a mixture of colouring materials, clay, lubricant, and binder. They are harder than chalks or pastels and thus provide a good way of making strong, clean images.

Erasers are an essential piece of extra equipment for pencil work, and there are various types. Soft ones which crumble when used avoid any risk of damage to the paper, and kneadable erasers or putty rubbers can be formed into points for creating small areas of highlight. Solid erasers can be carved into shapes using a blade.

PENCIL EFFECTS

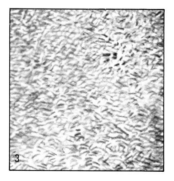
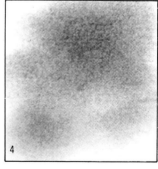

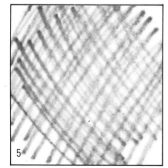

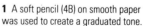

1 A soft pencil (4B) on smooth paper was used to create a graduated tone.

2 The same 4B pencil produces a coarser effect on rough paper.

3 This stippled effect was made using various coloured pencils, with the strokes lightly blended together.

4 A very soft effect can be made by blending coloured pencil dust.

5 These soft, faded lines are created by drawing coloured pencil over wet watercolour paper.

6 Highlights are produced by erasing parts of the pencil design.

Above Stuart Bodek (A. P.) *Laughing Gas* (detail): pencil

Laughing Gas (Detail)

This is an example of a very tight pencil technique, in which the accuracy of the draughtsmanship matches the precise nature of the reference. The brief demanded total authenticity, and all the elements of the illustration were photographed.

Within very precise outlines, a wide range of tones was achieved, using only one grade of pencil – in this case an F. The subtlety of manipulation and the patient build-up of marks created a great deal of variety over the image.

Young Masai Cattle Minder

This sketch was made on location using a 2B Progresso – a solid graphite stick. This provides a larger area of graphite than a pencil, enabling the type of line to be varied very fluently by slightly altering the angle at which it is held. Further variation was achieved by adjusting the pressure; the light lines were made by just skimming the graphite stick across the surface.

Speed of working was essential in this drawing, since the character and main qualities of the unposed figures had to be caught quickly. A minimum of marks was made, with emphasis on the most important areas; for example, the head, where the nature of the pencil allowed very free and fluid marks.

Dark Flight

This is a black and white book cover illustration, for which a rough design was made and the reference was then very accurately researched. All the separate elements were then assembled on tracing paper in conformity with the original rough. The design was then transferred by rubbing pencil on the back of the tracing paper, laying it down on a sheet of smooth, heavy cartridge (drawing) paper and drawing over the lines of the design, which then appeared as faint graphite marks on the paper.

The outline was drawn with a 3H pencil, and the tones were built up carefully and precisely with an HB pencil. This method necessitated frequent use of a scalpel blade (X-acto knife) to ensure a point sharp enough to give a consistently fine mark. For positively dark areas a softer pencil was used – a 2B.

The precise passages, the face, for example, were completed first leaving the broader areas, such as the smoke, till last. Finally, the whole image was reviewed, and fine adjustments made to the facial tones.

Top Jane Mitchell (S.) *Young Masai Cattle Minder:* pencil, 9 × 7 in (23 × 18 cm)

Above Biz Hull (A. P.) *Dark Flight:* pencil, 6 × 6 in (15 × 15 cm)

Old Devotions

This book jacket was drawn using a very tight pencil technique, and when the original artwork was reduced for the cover, the individual pencil marks became indistinct.

Creating a very dark area is one of the trickier aspects of coloured pencil technique. The dark colour here was built up by using several thin layers of different colours – blue, brown, and black – thus avoiding the dead look of black used on its own. The use of layers also avoided the patchy look that can occur when a dark colour is used by itself.

The background to the brick area was first covered in a pale colour, after which the individual bricks were worked up with a variety of colours, the end result looking somewhat like a watercolour.

Because this was a slow and delicate process, the area of the drawing beneath the artist's hand was masked off with paper, both to prevent oils from the skin from spoiling the surface and to prevent smudging. The risk of smudging was further minimized by spraying on fixative as soon as a part of the image had been satisfactorily established. An eraser was in constant use to keep the paper clean – essential in an image where the white paper forms a substantial part of the design.

Above Biz Hull (A. P.) *Old Devotions:* coloured pencil, 9½ × 6½ in (24 × 17 cm)

Left Biz Hull (A. P.)
Andrew and Tobias:
coloured pencil, 7 × 8½
in (18 × 22 cm)

Right Chris Riddell (A. P.)
Ellen: coloured pencil,
12 × 8 in (30 × 20 cm)

Ellen

In this, one of a series of book covers which had featured a border, the artist followed suit and produced two pieces of artwork, one for the border of bricks and one for the inset image.

The brief was relatively loose, the artist simply being given the manuscript to read. He chose to illustrate the rather drab setting of the story instead of providing clues to the dramatic developments, which would have been an alternative approach. Having decided on an image he then selected coloured pencils as the medium best suited to it. First, he made an underdrawing in black ink, and the image was then constructed in coloured pencil, using the toned paper as the basic midtone. The toned paper also allowed him to create the impression of a window at night by applying light strokes of the chalky crayon over it.

This is essentially a tonal composition in which the marks of the pencils are important, so that the finished result is clearly a drawing, retaining a visual vibrancy, rather than a meticulous piece of realism.

Andrew and Tobias

The clients required a loose pencil image for this book about a pair of twins separated from birth. The artist took her own photographs as reference for the figures and used printed reference material for the stately home in the background.

The planned composition was transferred to cartridge (drawing) paper for the execution of the final artwork, and the outline was re-established with a 3H pencil. The colour was worked in Caran d'Ache pencils, and the first area of colour to be dealt with was the flesh, since in such an obviously figurative piece the heads and the hands form the focus of attention.

PASTEL AND CRAYON

Pastels are made by compressing powdered pigment into stick shapes with a binding medium which holds the pigment together. The range of shades in any one colour is created by the addition of a filler such as chalk for the pale shades, and black pigment for the dark ones.

Since it is pure pigment, pastel has some claim to be the oldest colouring medium of all, but it reached its peak as a medium in 18th-century France, where it was much used for portraiture, with line and blended areas skilfully exploited. Toward the end of the 19th century Edgar Degas further exploited the qualities of pastel, using it almost as a painting medium by mixing it with turpentine, which allowed considerable over-drawing.

The pastel process, although no brushes are used, is essentially more akin to painting than to drawing. The chief advantage for the illustrator is that there is no liquid medium and hence no drying time to consider.

The range of tints of any colour is vast. (Usually 0 is the lightest and 8 is the darkest, but different manufacturers have different grading systems.) An individual artist will make a selection according to his or her preferred colour and tonal range. In this respect pastel is quite unlike the paint media, in which an infinite variety of colours can be mixed from a relatively small range; pastels cannot be pre-mixed, so a basic working palette should include a light, middle, and dark tone of each selected colour.

Supports ranging from canvas to sandpaper have been used for pastel, but paper is the most generally favoured, and there are many papers to choose from, specially made for pastels. Where the image is likely to be rather loose free tinted papers are normally used, since these influence and contribute to the appearance of the final work. A variety of tones can be achieved by treating the tinted paper as a mid-tone, and a coloured paper can be used as a key for the rest of the colour scheme.

Right Edgar Degas *Après le Bain, Femme s'Essuyant* This pastel drawing gives a strong effect of texture. A wide variety of marks were used, from short pressured strokes to long sweeping lines. In some areas the pastels were worked in open, webbed layers, allowing the underlying colours to read through.

Above Jean-Baptiste Perronneau *Girl with a Kitten* This portrait shows a very delicate, heavily blended use of pastel.

The type of mark made with pastel is dictated by which part of the stick is used. Broad sweeps are made by using the side of the pastel, fine lines by using the tip, and tones are varied by altering the pressure. Individual marks can be laid side by side or blended together with a torchon (stump) or with the fingers, but blending must be done with care to avoid smeary areas. Textures can be produced by the juxtaposition of different strokes, such as dashes and dots, and interesting effects can be created by layers of cross-hatching.

The powdery surface of the pastel tends to fall off the paper easily, but it can be sprayed with fixative to prevent accidental smudging. Fixative can also be used during the course of a work to isolate an area so that further marks can be made on top. Fixative does tend to darken the colours slightly, and can cause blotches if used incautiously, so proceed with care.

Oil pastels, which are made by grinding pigment in oil, come in a much smaller range of colours, but they are clear and bright. They have the advantage of needing no fixing, and can be mixed and manipulated on the paper by blending with turpentine to create broad, painterly effects.

PASTEL TECHNIQUES

LAYING AN AREA OF TONE **1** Draw in a small area of thick colour using the blunted end of the pastel.

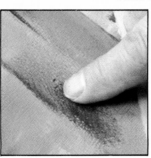

2 Use the fingertip to spread the colour over the required area.

3 With a tortillon, work the colour into a more accurate shape.

CREATING SURFACE TEXTURE
1 Coloured paper reads through the grainy texture of pastel work to create an extra tone.

2 Mix pastel colours using open strokes to allow the colours to work together.

3 Contrast hatching with blocks of solid colour to create a varied texture.

OIL PASTEL WITH TURPENTINE WASH
1 Use a brush moistened with turpentine to create a coloured wash.

2 Apply soft strokes of pastel to build up a layer of textured colour.

Left Debbie Hinks (A. P.) *Girl Reclining:*
pastel, 20 × 30 in (51 × 76 cm)

Above *Girl Reclining* (detail)

Debbie Hinks (A. P.) *Delta of Venus:* pastel, 30 × 20 in (76 × 51 cm)

Girl Reclining

In this free and direct drawing the outline was established on coloured paper using pastel with no preliminary pencil drawing. The bold, flowing line is characteristic of the medium, which requires some assurance since it allows for little correction. The line is dictated by the arc made by the hand around the wrist and the sweep of the arm from the point of the elbow. This way of working necessitates large sheets of paper; pastel is not a medium suited to fine finger-controlled manipulation on much smaller pieces of paper.

Large areas were rapidly blocked in, using both the tip of the pastel in a hatching technique and the side of the stick to make broad, flat strokes. The gentle, graduated fading of colour into the tint of the paper was achieved by rubbing first with the thumb and then with an eraser. An eraser used directly on the "neat" pastel would be both ineffective and messy, since it would merely smear the colour without erasing it. Torchons (stumps) and cotton buds (swabs) were also used for blending.

As the artist finished each area she sprayed it with fixative. In this way she was able to work on other parts of the image with no risk of spoiling the completed sections. It also allowed her to add final touches, such as highlights, to established areas.

Delta of Venus

The outline was first drawn with Conté pencil, after which the artist concentrated her efforts on the face and parts of the body, blending the pastel to create a flesh-like softness. The variation, around the eyes in particular, was created by building up layers of different-coloured pastels, fixing each one before laying the next.

The pure colours of pastels lend themselves to the production of strong pattern, and pattern has been exploited in the background of this picture, where the design of the kimono was transferred to form a back-drop against which the grey of the paper "reads" as a flat shape.

Ice Cream

In this piece the artist has used oil pastel, which he describes as "like drawing with a piece of chocolate" because of the way it melts as it runs over the paper. However, it is in many ways a clean medium to work with, since it is not soluble, except in turpentine, and thus does not smear or rub off, as ordinary pastel does. Another advantage is that it reduces well and retains the liveliness of the handling.

The image here is a spontaneous one, made with no attempt to be fussy about correcting mistakes, except in one section, which was corrected by sticking a piece of paper over it and reworking on top. Such repair work is rarely noticeable in reproduction.

Dance Practice

This rapidly executed image was done on a smooth shiny paper, and the overall colour effect of the background was created by scribbling over the area with a mixture of crayons and then rubbing down the marks with tissue paper to blend them. The figures were drawn directly onto this base colour and then smudged to create the effect of motion.

Above Nick Sharratt *Ice-Cream:* oil pastel, 28 × 18 in (71 × 46 cm)

Left Nick Sharratt *Dance Practice:* wax oil crayon, 18 × 23 in (46 × 58 cm)

PEN AND INK

The range of pens and allied implements available to the artist today is vast. The reed pen makes a hard, powerful mark which is affected by the spread of the split which carries the ink. The marks made by the quill pen depend largely on the type of feather used and the way it is cut, and it can be shaped and re-shaped by careful cutting. The standard dip pen is varied by virtue of the very large assortment of different steel nibs which can be used, all of which are quickly fitted into the pen-holder. Both the fountain pen and the technical pen are much used for illustration, but specially formulated free-flowing inks are necessary.

The pen was used as an illustration medium in medieval books and as a tool for scientific observation during the Renaissance. The strong contrast of black and white provided by pen and ink was popular in 18th- and 19th-century illustration work, being first printed by hand and later by photo-mechanical means.

Paper is the only surface suitable for pen and ink work, and soft textures are best avoided, since they are likely to tear and block the nib. Also, if the paper is too porous the ink could bleed, marring the clarity of the line.

Pen and ink work, with its naturally flowing line, creates immediate and powerful visual statements in both line and tone, which takes the form of dots, dashes, hatching and cross-hatching. Particularly deep black marks can be made by using Indian ink, which is a mixture of carbon with binders. It is sold in two forms: waterproof, which, when dry, is not soluble in water, and non-waterproof, which can be washed away when dry. Both can be diluted with water.

Ink drawings are often combined with washes of coloured inks or watercolour. In both cases the preliminary ink outline must be allowed to dry before the washes are applied, or alternatively the ink outlines can be drawn in as a final stage after the washes have dried.

Corrections to an ink image are not easy, though dry ink can sometimes be scraped off with a blade if the paper is thick enough to withstand such treatment, and careful use of an eraser can be effective in modifying an area.

Top William Hogarth *Idle Apprentices at Play in a Churchyard* The use of ink and wash was ideally suited to Hogarth's bold, satirical cartoons.

Above Aubrey Beardsley illustration from *The Rape of the Lock* Beardsley's use of decorative line work and stippling in this pen and ink drawing is typical of his rather stylized images.

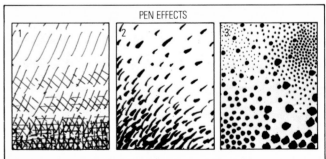

PEN EFFECTS

Above A wide range of tonal effects can be produced with ink, including the following: **1** Hatching and crosshatching **2** Dashes **3** Stippling

The Devil's Looking Glass

For this book cover, the client specified a grainy moonlight scene, to give a sinister effect to the college building.

The preliminary drawing was traced onto the paper, and the image was developed with a fine technical pen. The drawing consisted of hatching strokes and carefully controlled stippling; larger areas were blocked in using a brush, the stars being drawn around before the sky was painted.

Since no indication of the type area had been given, the artist left a bleed top and bottom so that the designer could put the lettering in either area.

Clive Sinclair

The clients had requested a gentle caricature of the subject of the book surrounded by his creations, and they supplied photographs of Clive Sinclair; the artist found his own reference for the hardware. The original idea showed Sinclair perched on top of a pile of his inventions, but the clients considered this too flippant, possibly even offensive, so this second version was done, featuring the same portrait but this time amid a landscape of his products.

The artist drew a preparatory design, but in order to retain an element of spontaneity in the finished piece he redrew the image rather than transferring it by using a light box.

Wherever a quantity of water is used for washes, paper should be pre-stretched, but in this case the image was only to be tinted, using relatively little water, so it was not necessary. A brief indication of shapes in pencil was followed by a thorough construction of forms and tones in pen and ink. The pencil was then rubbed out and watercolour washed on, quite thinly in order not to obscure the image in any way.

Above left Bill Gregory (A. P.) *The Devil's Looking Glass:* pen and ink, 8 × 5 (20 × 13 cm)

Above right Chris Riddell (A. P.) *Clive Sinclair:* pen and ink with watercolour, 9 × 10 in (23 × 25 cm)

Are You Good Enough for their Son?

This illustration provides an example of the positive, and very uniform line produced by a technical pen. Single areas of pure watercolour were painted on when the ink was dry, and lines of felt-tip pen added.

St James's Church

This image was created entirely with coloured inks and demonstrates the bright luminosity which is their main characteristic, quite different from the effect of watercolour. The inks were applied with a sable brush and adjusted while still wet by dragging a fine sponge across the surface. In some places they were allowed to merge while wet, but in others they were imposed on dry layers, giving a lucid, glazed effect. Fine adjustments were also made using coloured pencils and black ink.

Right David Watson *St James Church:* ink, 8½ × 11 in (21.5 × 29 cm)

Left Nick Sharratt *Are You Good Enough for their Son?:* pen and ink with watercolour, 3 × 7 in (8 × 18 cm)

MARKER PENS

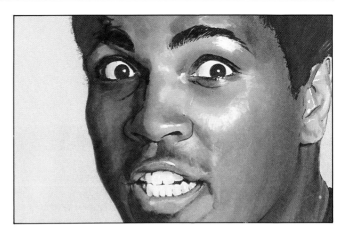

Ali

Marker pens are available in a wide range of colours and sizes, with various nib shapes including fine points, fine cylinder-shaped heads, blunt bullet-like points, and the popular and versatile wedge shape. The inks, either permanent (spirit-based) or water soluble, are specially formulated to flow easily and dry rapidly and are especially noted for their clarity of colour.

Markers, used simply for making lines or as a means of filling in areas of an image, are extremely convenient implements, involving no mess and requiring no other medium in their application.

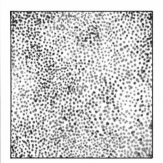 

EFFECTS WITH MARKERS Fine, multi-coloured marker pen dots create a pointillist effect **left** A mottled effect is produced by spraying a water-based marker design with a spirit solution **right**

Boat

This story-board image, deprived of its cardboard frame, allows us to "see behind" the smooth image. The individual strokes of the marker are clearly visible, as is the process of mixing.

This is an example of a highly finished storyboard image executed with markers containing spirit-based inks. The rough drawing was placed on a light box with a sheet of layout paper over it, and a thin nylon-tipped pen was used to trace a fine black outline. The artist began by developing the most difficult parts first – the eyes and mouth – since if he made an error at this stage only a little work would have been wasted. He established the mid tones first, progressing to the darks, and the highlights were created where possible by working around white paper. In some areas this was not feasible, so bleed-proof white was used.

A range of subtle marks was made by using old, dry marker pens, and these were pulled together and blended by flowing a mid-tone over them, using a very wet marker. The variability of flow needs to be constantly tested on scraps of paper or unwanted effects can occur.

A wide range of tones and colours was created by the overlap of the translucent inks and in order to create large areas of pure, flat colour the felt wadding was pulled from inside the marker bottle and used to create a "wash" – a technique demanding both skill and practice.

Top Kevin Tweddell (A. P.) *Ali:* marker pen, 6 × 8 in (15 × 20 cm)

Left Kevin Tweddell (A. P.) *Boat:* marker pen, 6 × 8 in (15 × 20 cm)

SCRAPERBOARD

Scraperboard provides a method of making white designs on black by carving or scratching a specially prepared surface with a sharp blade. Often used to imitate the qualities of woodcuts and wood engraving, scraperboard can create distinctive effects of its own, which are unlike any other technique.

The special triangular blades used for this work are fitted into an ordinary pen-holder. The blade enables a variety of marks to be made: the tip produces a thin line, while a thicker one is made by using the side. The techniques most often used are hatching and cross-hatching, and corrections are easily made by painting Indian ink over the lines, so in effect the image is infinitely adjustable.

The preparatory drawing for this image was traced, and transferred onto the black scraperboard, with the outline just established in a very thin line scratched on the surface. Then, starting with the main features of the design, the artist began to carve into the surface more boldly to establish strong contrasts of black and white. In this case the marks left between the strokes of the blade were purposely allowed to remain, since the artist felt they added "colour" to the otherwise stark areas of white.

The very fine diamond shapes and the broader marks of the bed show the delicacy and pattern variety that can be produced using this medium. The surface of the board, where left untouched, provides a strong statement of "night".

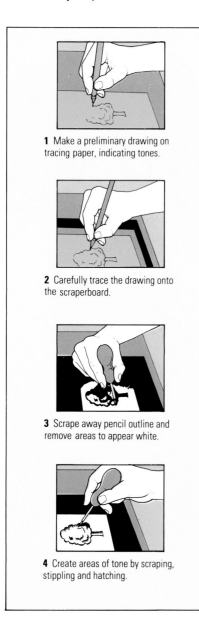

1 Make a preliminary drawing on tracing paper, indicating tones.

2 Carefully trace the drawing onto the scraperboard.

3 Scrape away pencil outline and remove areas to appear white.

4 Create areas of tone by scraping, stippling and hatching.

Above Jane Smith *Boy Dreaming:* scraperboard, 4½ × 3½ in (11 × 9 cm)

WATERCOLOUR

Watercolour paints are made from finely ground pigment mixed with gum arabic, and their hallmark is translucence. They can be diluted with large quantities of water, producing a colour so pale that it is little more than a stain on the paper, or used with little water to produce a vivid colour. The way the white paper reflects back through the transparent paint produces a clarity of hue that is unique to watercolour. It must always be worked from light to dark, building up the darkest colours by means of successive layers, or washes.

Watercolour has a long history as a medium for tinting drawings, but the watercolour technique as we know it today did not come into prominence until the late 18th century, with the landscapes of the "English School". The medium has been popular with artists ever since, both as a particularly sympathetic way of rendering atmospheric effects and as a way of producing clean, subtle colour. The invention in the 19th century of the three-colour half-tone printing process meant that illustrations could now be printed in colour, and consequently watercolour became an important commercial medium, much used by book illustrators.

It is a versatile medium, allowing both broad expressive statements and fine, meticulous "dry" brush work. A positive advantage for the illustrator is the relatively rapid drying time; a slight drawback is the comparatively limited tonal range, but the innate delicacy of colour more than compensates for this. Watercolour dries considerably lighter than it appears when wet, so some practice is needed before the strength of colours or tones can be accurately assessed.

The support for watercolour is paper, and there is a wide variety of papers, both hand- and machine-made, manufactured for it. Rough papers allow a free use of

TESTING FOR STAINING POWER **1** Paint a small patch of each colour on the required type of paper.

2 When the paint is dry, work over each area with a clean, wet brush.

3 Using a very wet sponge, wipe the paper with clean water to remove the paint.

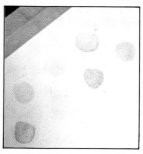

4 Once the paper has completely dried the colours with the deepest staining power are revealed.

Left Thomas Girton *Appledore* Only five colours were used in this watercolour. Superimposed washes produced the subtle tones, and white gouache was used to highlight the facades of the buildings.

STRETCHING PAPER **1** Check the watermark for the right side of the paper.

2 Trim the paper allowing a margin of clear board for the gummed paper to adhere to.

3 Soak the paper in a tray of clean water. The time allowed varies according to the type of paper (check with your supplier).

4 Measure out four lengths of gummed paper to the size of your board.

5 Drain the paper, and place right-side up on your board. Stick one side to the board with gummed paper.

6 Anchor the opposite side of the paper, and then the remaining two sides, keeping the paper flat at all times.

7 Finally secure the paper with a thumbtack in each corner, and allow it to dry naturally. The paper will dry tight and smooth.

washes and impart their own textural qualities to the finished piece. The smoother papers permit a more accurate placing of colour but do not accept wet washes readily and demand a very deliberate application of paint as they do not hold the pigment so firmly. Heavy papers or watercolour boards (thin watercolour paper mounted on cardboard) can be painted on directly, but medium and thin papers require stretching or they will buckle when wet.

The paints themselves are available in various forms. Tubes are ideal for setting out the large quantities of paint needed for washes; pans are convenient in many ways, but their surface can become very messy unless one is careful to clean the brush before loading with colour. Bottles of liquid watercolour complete with dropper provide an immediate and clean source of strong colour. When using these it is advisable to have two containers of water, one for loading the brush for mixing, and one for cleaning the brush before changing colour.

The basic and most characteristic application of watercolour is the wash; this is the covering of an area, large or small, with a perfectly flat colour. This is done with a fully loaded brush on either dry or dampened paper, taking a line of paint from one side to the other, and then another one just below in the opposite direction. Almost inevitably where the brush comes to a halt there will be a blob of colour, but this is easily remedied by squeezing out the brush and running it over the offending area, allowing the brush to soak up the liquid. It is essential to use good-quality brushes for laying washes, for only these will have sufficient body to carry enough paint for the wash.

If a shape to be covered by a wash is dampened accurately with the water, the colour will flow only to that particular area, and the paint laid on the damp-ened surface can be moved around the shape until an even covering is achieved. The mobile nature of this process allows subtle, almost indistinguishable grada-tions to be produced, and if necessary the whole sur-face of the paper can be loaded with water, using a sponge or a small hand sprayer. The build-up of thin washes one over another creates a luminous effect. A thin wash is produced by lifting off some of the paint, either by allowing a wash to dry and then scrubbing over it with clean water, or by blotting a wet wash off with tissue or blotting paper. Another wash can then be applied to the reduced area and the process repeated. On the rough papers the "peaks" of the textured sur-face will be lighter than the "valleys" between, which gives an attractive flecked effect.

Soft fuzzy shapes with indistinct outlines can be created by making fully loaded brush strokes on wet paper or still moist washes, called working wet into wet. The variations are limitless; permutations of dampness of surface and intensity of brush marks create endless variety.

LAYING A WASH AGAINST A DEFINED EDGE **1** Draw your outline and dampen the paper up to this edge.

2 Work the colour in to the dampened area, allowing the paint to spread up to the outline.

3 The area below can now be covered with a wash.

Blotting paper can be used to soak up excess paint to create a thin wash, and also to control the actual paint flow.

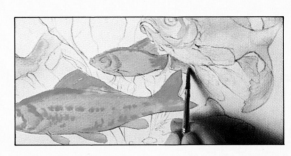

WORKING WET INTO WET To create the softly blended effect in the detailing of the gills, fins and scales the darker paint was applied before the basic wash had completely dried.

Dry brush work is done by squeezing a loaded brush between the fingers or partially drying it with a rag or paper towels until it retains only a little paint. If using fingers make sure you wash them before starting the work. Some practice is needed to ensure that there is just the right amount of paint on the brush – too little and it will make no marks; too much and the result will simply be a wash. The idea of this technique is to leave tiny lines of paint on the surface of the paper, and it is an excellent method both for creating clear, unmuddied darks and for drawing fine lines as though with a pencil. Stippling with a fine dry brush can also create interesting texture and colour effects – dots of separate colour blend in the viewer's eye to present subtle hues. Used delicately with pale colours, dry brush work is a way of correcting uneven washes, the fine hatching strokes merging with the edges of the patchy wash.

Watercolours can be corrected by lightening areas with a soft eraser or by thoroughly wetting with clean water and either dabbing with tissue or scrubbing with a brush. Small areas can be wiped out with a cotton bud (swab) dipped in clean water. Such correction is generally only successful on good-quality watercolour paper.

White highlights can be produced in solid areas by first reserving the required shapes by painting them with masking fluid, by the careful use of a sharp blade, or, again, by wiping with cotton buds (swabs). Both the latter techniques should be reserved for small areas only.

DRY BRUSH WORK **1** Load the brush with paint and remove the surplus on blotting paper or with a rag.

2 To apply, fan out the bristles of the brush between finger and thumb and work over the required area.

3 For dry brush work, use either a chisel-shaped brush or fan out a round hair brush.

Sheep Market

In examining the procedures adopted by Jackie Campbell in the painting, *Sheep Market,* we see a rather precise technique which makes use of many of the basic watercolour methods.

A number of photographs and sketches were made, "on site", and from this information the artist made roughs to explore various groupings and to experiment with the use of colour and texture. In the sketch illustrated here the outline was drawn with pencil and a dip pen and then filled in with watercolour washes. The figures and sheep have become stylized in the process, and the focus is on the details, so that the painting is a kind of decorative catalogue of information – the boots, the shepherd's crook, the man bidding.

The composition was arrived at by making tracings of specific figures and passages and then juggling them within the planned dimensions of the picture – like a mobile jigsaw puzzle. When a satisfactory arrangement had been achieved, a single overall tracing was made; this was transferred to a heavy watercolour paper, and the drawing was made in pencil.

The initial washes were applied using a lifting technique. With brush in one hand and tissue in the other the artist applied a flood of colour and then, dabbing with absorbent tissue, reduced the intensity. The desired tint was thus achieved by a succession of thin veils of colour. When this had dried, a dry brush technique was used for defining the detail. For the ground of the market a hog's hair brush was used with the bare minimum of paint to produce a stippled effect.

Some areas of the image were adjusted by the appli-

cation of further washes after the detail had been put in. The fuzzy wood grain of the auctioneer's desk was achieved by going over the dry brush detail with a wash, which softened the line. The character to the top right of the picture was made to recede slightly by being covered with a wash, and the distant figures, which were felt by the artist to be too strong, were adjusted by the use of an opaque mist of very thin white gouache.

Fishes and Dogs

These sketches by a scientific illustrator were attempts to capture the liveliness and spirit of the subjects as back-up to her accurate and detailed studies on their exact physical appearance. The artist wanted to capture the way the animal moved in the sketches of dogs.

The loose technique of working wet into wet often creates happy accidents, with the uncontrolled bleeding of the paint expressing the feeling of movement

very aptly. The fish were approached in the same way, and the artist used coloured pencils in a free manner as well as flowing washes of watercolour.

The information gained from sketches like these, in combination with accurate anatomical detail, enables the artist to create convincing scientific images which express the animate qualities of the subject, rather than being pieces of frozen accuracy.

Above left Jackie Campbell *Sheep Market:* watercolour, 15 × 19½ in (38 × 49 cm)

Above Jane Reynolds (S.) *Fishes:* watercolour, 9 × 6½ in (23 × 16 cm)

Far left Preliminary colour visual for *Sheep Market*

Left Jane Reynolds (S.) *Dogs:* watercolour

Right Jackie Campbell
The Old Man and the Sea:
watercolour, 15 × 10 in
(38 × 25 cm)

The Old Man and the Sea

This illustration featuring the capture of the marlin from Ernest Hemingway's *The Old Man and the Sea* allowed a watercolour that is essentially imaginative, a response to the text rather than the product of research and reference.

For the artist the striking theme was the awe felt by the man for the magnificent fish and his respect for the sea itself. Her response was to stylize not only the elements of the image but also the manner of painting them. The water is rendered as pattern, and the anatomically disproportionate figure of the man is treated with an enamel-like distinction between colours and tones.

The spray effect was established at the outset by the use of masking fluid and the washes for the sea were painted over. The striped pattern of the water in the right-hand corner was obtained by linear washes of translucent watercolour and opaque gouache thinly applied. The fine lines over the whole image were made by the careful manipulation of a dry brush.

Camping Out

For this illustration a thorough "rough" was first completed, and then carefully-lit photographs were taken for reference, from a tent set up in the artist's living-room. The broad areas of the composition were drawn on the hot-pressed (smooth) watercolour board chosen for the painting, and then the negatives of the colour film were projected onto it and the image was drawn up in meticulous detail using a fine 0.3 pencil (mechanical lead-holder). To adjust the size of the images the projector was simply moved backwards or forwards.

The artist worked on individual parts in isolation, preferring to work up each area to its final state rather than broadly indicating the whole picture. He found that the satisfaction gained from a successful piece of painting acted as a spur to progress. A range of sable brushes was used, from a number 2 for blocking in areas to a tiny 000 for the very fine detail.

Wherever possible the intense colours of the photographic reference were matched in the strength of the paint, but really large areas necessitated the building up of colours from successive washes. Throughout the piece, the artist used spare strips of watercolour paper to check colour against colour.

The details on which the eye tends to focus were worked very finely, but on the less crucial areas the technique was looser, and the occasional chance effects often created by the watercolour technique were allowed to remain. Fine lines were achieved by painting the lines in white gouache and then quickly washing over with the appropriate colour; this is a more immediate method than trying to reserve fine lines by leaving white paper.

HOLIDAY HINTS FOR CHEEKY CHIMPS

Above John Marriott (A. P.) *Camping Out:* watercolour, 9½ × 12½ in (24 × 32 cm) The artist took his own photographic reference for the figures **top** before completing a colour visual **middle**.

GOUACHE

Gouache (or designer's colour) is basically the same as watercolour, but it is mixed with white pigment and extender, which makes it opaque. Opaque watercolour, also called body colour, has been used by artists since the 15th century, and today it is an important medium for the commercial artist because it can produce such bright, clear colours. Gouache paint, when dry, forms a positive film of colour quite different from the stain-like effect produced by watercolour, and independent of the paper beneath it. A particularly useful characteristic is that it can be manipulated to produce flat areas of colour, and its consistency enables accurate straight lines to be made with a brush or ruling-pen. Sharp, hard divisions of solid colour are particularly associated with gouache paint, but many more free and immediate techniques can also be used, such as liquid mixtures in which the brush-strokes are visible, loose hatching which allows the ground to show through and wet paint worked into wet paint. Whatever the method of application the striking quality is the paint's ability to provide strong contrasts of tone and colour.

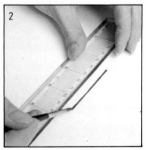

The essential quality of gouache is its opacity, which can be exploited to produce areas of flat colour **1** and also very fine lines **2**.

Any of the paper and boards used for watercolour are suitable for gouache, and since the medium is opaque, tinted papers can also be used. Corrections can be made by re-wetting the area with a tissue, scraping, or simply painting over an unsatisfactory passage.

Choirboys

For the design of this Christmas card the artist began directly with brush and paint; preliminary pencil drawing was restricted to thumbnail sketches on scraps of paper. The technique used at this stage was quite loose, in order to establish quickly the general areas and forms, and the colours were deliberately left imperfectly mixed, giving an effect of streaked brushmarks.

The second stage was one of consolidation. The ele-

Above Annette Alcock (D. W. D.) *Choirboys:* gouache, 7 × 5 in (18 × 13 cm) The artist initially sketched the design of the card in a very loose form **top left**, before executing a more planned visual **top right**.

Right Stephen Adams (A. P.) *Biscuits and Cakes:* gouache, 5 × 7 in (13 × 18 cm)

ments indicated in the first image were re-examined and placed in a more planned way, with more consideration for both the overall design and the individual shapes. This part of the process necessitated three attempts before the artist was satisfied with the design.

In the final, finished artwork stage, the brushwork was more closely controlled, but still painted directly with no preliminary drawing. The colours used in a milky consistency, were worked from dark to light, exploiting the covering power of gouache, and sharp contrasts were used in the creation of pattern. Throughout the work, care was taken to produce crisp and unmuddied colours which would reproduce well, and the liveliness of the execution is reflected in the clearly evident brushmarks. Whenever the paint became too thick or the image needed correcting wet tissue paper was dabbed over the offending area and the paint removed.

Biscuits and Cakes

The objects were drawn as a still life on tracing paper, and when the image was sufficiently refined it was transferred to the painting surface using a graphite paper. Where the traced-through line was too strong the marks were softened with an eraser to avoid the danger of the line showing through the paint.

The board used was an illustration board, which provided the smooth surface needed for this gouache technique. The artist kept the image light and clean by working from the line tones toward the dark, but adding the highlights last. Creamy opaque paint was used for the main body of the work, with thinner mixtures reserved for the subtle changes of tone.

The translucent cherries were created using three tones, a restriction which ensured a crisper, less fussy build up of form, and the small tonal changes were added as thin washes over the top. The white highlight was added very quickly to avoid muddying the clear, light area.

Throughout the work various improvements were made, for example, the crumbling side of the biscuit was made to crumble tidily. The colours reflected in the jam were ignored, as were the unnecessary shadows, which tend to look dirty if painted in, and continual adjustments in the interests of clarity were made. Where in reality the objects would merge, with spatial distinctions becoming unclear, the artist accentuated contrasts of light and dark in order to establish the separate existence of each item.

Packet Foods

This bold design was a response to a brief requiring the image to be colourful and strongly patterned. It was painted on a grey paper – left unpainted on the dustbin (trashcan) – using gouache mixed with very little water. The bright colours thus produced add to the effect of pattern.

The artist developed the painting as it progressed rather than restricting herself to a tight master-plan. For example, the white border was an afterthought, which allowed the image to dissolve into the text on the printed page rather than sitting in its own rectangle. In this case white acrylic was used instead of gouache, so that the red could be added with no fear of adulteration; acrylic dries very quickly and is not soluble in water.

Above Jane Smith *Packet Foods:* gouache, 4½ × 4½ in (11 × 11 cm)

Fairground Horse

Once the drawing had been established on the paper, the different areas of colour were defined as flat, solid mid-tones. The variety within each colour was achieved by stippling first with dark tones of the colour and then with light ones, after which dots were blended with a brush loaded with clean water. The fading at the edges was obtained by working white into the image.

On the smooth areas of the image, for example the body of the horse, untextured transitions were achieved by laying on two colours next to each other and running over the junction with clean water.

Right Susan Robertson (D. W. D.) *Fairground Horse:* gouache, 3 × 4 in (7.5 × 10 cm)

Below Stephen Adams (A. P.) *Butterflies:* gouache, 8 × 16 in (20 × 40.5 cm)

Butterflies

The butterflies were treated in a strong, intense manner, working from light to dark, and the background, which was visually less important, was painted with thinned gouache in a watercolour technique with no overpainting. The lack of detailed contrast has successfully set it back in space. Thinned gouache gives a pastel effect quite different from that of a watercolour wash.

EGG TEMPERA

Above Duccio di Buoninsegna *Madonna and Child* Quattrocento triptych Tempera on a polished white gesso ground was used to achieve the luminous quality of the paint.

Egg tempera is a paint made by grinding pigment in the yolk of an egg. This can be, and often is, done by the artist, but there are also proprietary brands of ready-made tempera.

This was the paint used for medieval frescoes and altar-pieces, in which the figures were carefully modelled using small strokes of the brush over a detailed underpainting. Tempera is a tricky medium to use, as it cannot be moved or manipulated, and it was supplanted by the more versatile oil paint as the common painting medium from the 16th century. However, its qualities are still admired by some artists today, and it has been used for both illustration and painting.

It is applied with water as a diluent, but once dry it becomes insoluble, thus allowing further layers to be added. This layering technique creates a characteristic intensity of colour, but also demands a systematic approach on the part of the artist since the rapid drying precludes any blending of colour or tone.

Ideally, tempera paintings are executed on gesso panels (panels coated with a mixture of glue and chalk) which provide a brilliant white, smooth and absorbent surface, but good-quality watercolour paper or watercolour boards can be used very successfully.

The traditional process was to transfer a very accurate drawing to the surface and then to build up the image using short, narrow brushstrokes laid down parallel to each other. Often an underpainting would be done in monochrome, usually green or greeny-brown, and the final colours established as thin washes. But tempera can be used in a much freer way; for example, thin paint can be washed on with a wide brush; textures can be created by overlapping hatching in different colours; and thick mixtures can be applied with a coarse brush or even a knife, just as oils or acrylics often are.

CREATING TEXTURE
1 Using a fine brush, apply thin strokes of paint in a contrasting colour onto a thin wash.

2 Repeat the process of crosshatching to create a richer texture, building up as many layers as are required.

MAKING EGG YOLK BINDER **1** Crack an egg and separate the yolk by allowing the white to drain through the fingers.

2 Dry the yolk on a sheet of absorbent paper, then cut the yolk sack and allow the contents to run into a glass jar.

3 Slowly add distilled water and stir until the mixture reaches a consistency of thin cream. Strain into another glass jar.

MIXING PIGMENT PASTE with egg yolk binder **1** Mix a quantity of pigment paste and egg yolk binder on a paper palette.

2 To test the mixture for binding, put a little paint on a piece of clean glass and allow to dry.

3 Lift the paint with a palette knife. If it forms a skin it is ready for use; if it crumbles add more egg to the mixture.

Still Life

The image was made up from several photographs taken of a French graveyard which included tomb ornaments made of non-perishable materials such as metal and glass. The central element was enlarged to a 10 × 8 in print size and a full-scale drawing was made which was then traced and transferred to a gesso panel using graphite paper.

Throughout the painting, proprietary tempera colours were used in pure, unmixed form. The dark areas were laid in first to establish the tonal key, and then the large area in the lower part of the picture was built up using violet, burnt sienna and ultramarine flooded on in thin washes with ox-hair brushes. In other places the paint was used thick, and spread on with a knife; sometimes a sponge was used and sometimes paint was applied with a fingertip. The absorbency of the gesso caused the paint to dry very rapidly, thus allowing a rapid application of successive layers.

Particularly subtle colours were achieved by first painting on a colour and then covering it with white, after which another colour was applied on top, and so on. In these areas the paint was applied with a mouth diffuser and sponges, thus alternating the scumbling and glazing techniques. The dots which form the glass beads were applied with a round-headed brush – some in pure colour and some glazed over. The lettering was established early in pure white and amended as the image progressed.

Above Philip O'Reilly *Still Life:* egg tempera, 24 × 30 in (61 × 76 cm) The detail **left** shows the fine dot work highlighting the contours of the leaves.

OIL PAINT

Oil paint is made by grinding pigment in oil, and it is the oil content that gives the paint both its fluidity and its slow drying time, which allows the artist to manipulate and blend tones and colours.

It was first used in the 15th century as a medium for applying glazes over tempera paintings, and only really came into its own in the hands of 16th- and 17th-century painters such as Titian and Rubens, who used a more direct technique to exploit the thick, creamy nature of the paint. Among their prime concerns was the dramatic effect of lights and darks. The French Impressionists, for whom colour was all-important, employed a rainbow palette for their short strokes of pure colour which blended in the eye of the viewer – a technique known as optical mixing. In the work of Van Gogh and later artists, the brushstrokes themselves have a physical presence and form an important part of the image.

Oil paint is extremely versatile and can be applied thick or thin in an almost infinite variety of techniques, but for the illustrator the main drawback is the drying time.

Canvases and wooden panels are the traditional supports for oil painting. A priming coat is applied to form a ground – an isolating film which prevents the oil from soaking into the support and damaging both it and the paint layer. Both oil- and acrylic-based primers are available in artists' suppliers, or ready prepared canvases or canvas boards can be purchased.

The golden rule in oil painting is to work "fat over

GLAZING
1 Mix paint with turpentine and medium to a thin, oily consistency.

2 Apply the glaze to a dry underpainting to create a transparent film of colour.

3 This allows the underpainting to show through but effectively modifies the colour.

Norman Rockwell *The County Agricultural Agent* Rockwell perfected the use of oil techniques to produce an almost photographic clarity in this painting.

lean", which means that superimposed layers should have more oil in them than the layers underneath. The more oil used, the slower the drying time, and this method prevents the top layer from drying before the one underneath it, which could cause cracking.

Commercial tube paints are finely ground by mechanical means, and have extenders added to ensure a thick consistency. Paint can be used direct from the tube, but if it is diluted with turpentine or a mixture of turpentine and linseed oil more fluent brushmarks are obtained. Turpentine used alone hastens the rate of drying and produces a matt surface. Special painting media are made for techniques such as glazing, in which a transparent layer of paint is applied over a dry colour, producing a luminosity quite unlike the effect of the physical mixing of colours. Synthetic painting media are also available for use with oils as glaze diluents and as thickening gels, and some of these are specially formulated to speed up the paint's drying time.

A traditional procedure in oil painting is to start by drawing the image in charcoal or charcoal pencil (graphite pencil marks tend to reject oil paint) and then applying thin paint diluted with turpentine to make an underpainting – a broad treatment of the final image which indicates the shapes and tones of the finished painting. The painting can then be worked up and the forms and colours established by whatever technique the artist finds suitable to the subject. The stiff yet pliable nature of oil paint allows it to be applied in several different ways: the conventional brushes, there are specially designed painting knives, and paint can be squeezed on straight from the tube or wiped on with rags or the fingers. Brushes must be thoroughly cleaned in white (mineral) spirit and then in warm soapy water.

Cathedral

The artist used book references to work out the composition of this Christmas card as well as drawing a careful reconstruction of the cathedral in order to re-create detail not clearly visible in the photographs.

The drawing was transferred to an oil board, and a broad underpainting in grey-brown established the main shapes and tones, quickly covering the white of the primed board. The detail was painted with pure, unmixed colour, occasionally diluted with a little oil. The fine marks – for example, the snow around the wheel tracks – were picked out with small dots and dashes of unblended paint.

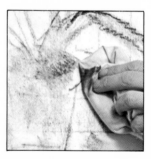
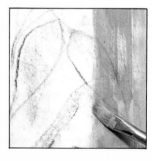

UNDERDRAWING WITH CHARCOAL
1 Create a free charcoal underdrawing, establishing line and tone.

2 Remove any loose charcoal dust by lightly wiping the surface with a rag.

3 Apply an underpainting with diluted colour, allowing the drawing to show through.

4 Using the underdrawing as a basic guide, fill in the basic shapes with solid colour.

5 The drawing is eventually disguised as the painting develops.

Above Bill Gregory (A. P.) *Cathedral:* oil paint, 14 × 18 in (35 × 46 cm)

BLENDING TONES OF COLOUR
1 Using a dry fan brush, work lightly over the join where the two tones meet. Wipe the brush at regular intervals.

2 Continue to work across the bands of colour, gradually progressing outwards.

3 This results in an area of soft tonal progression.

ACRYLIC

Acrylic paint is a mixture of pigments with synthetic resins, and is the product of specific industrial research. Such paints were used in the inter-war years, but it was only after the Second World War that they became available to the general public.

Acrylic colours are extremely versatile; heavily diluted they can be used like watercolour paints, but mixed with an acrylic medium they can be applied in thick impastos. They cannot, however, be pushed around the surface as oil paints can, for they dry extremely fast. This is a positive advantage to the illustrator as layer can be put over layer with little delay, and the toughness of the paint film prevents any damage to the underlying surface.

Acrylic can be used on all manner of surfaces – stretched canvas, panels, good-quality boards and paper. Canvas and wood panels will need priming, and acrylic gesso is made for this purpose. It is not actually gesso, but a brilliant white primer which provides the correct absorbency and tooth (key) for acrylic paints, and it can either be scraped on with a knife or applied with a broad brush. Boards and stretched paper can be painted on directly, but gesso thinned with water can be used to prime the surface if desired. Acrylic medium, which is transparent, also offers a good surface and is particularly useful when the artist wishes to retain the colour of the paper or cardboard. Grounds can be coloured by adding some acrylic colour to gesso primer or by brushing a very thin colour over it.

Corrections are usually made by overpainting with opaque paint, but thin washes can be removed using a fine abrasive sheet. Acrylic paints cannot be sponged off as they are impervious to water. Brushes used for work in this medium must be washed immediately after use, for paint allowed to dry on the brushes will ruin them.

The process of underpainting and overpainting described for oils can be achieved much more quickly with acrylics. Whether the preliminary painting is a monochrome indication or a broad underlay of colour it can be painted on within minutes. The *alla prima*, or direct, technique of oil painting, in which the aim is to

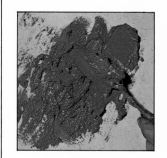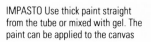

IMPASTO Use thick paint straight from the tube or mixed with gel. The paint can be applied to the canvas with a palette knife **1** to cover large areas, or with a brush for blobs of colour **2**.

achieve the final image with no preliminary underpainting, is also well suited to acrylic paint, because layers of paint can be applied in rapid succession.

A number of media are available which alter the appearance and handling qualities of the paint. Gloss medium imparts a shine akin to oil paint, while matt medium makes it resemble gouache paint. A retarder can be used to slow the drying time, while gel will

Left There is a wide selection of acrylic mediums which alter the basic opaque and dry qualities of the paint.

THICKENER

MATT MEDIUM

MODELLING PASTE

GEL MEDIUM

 TEXTURE PASTE

TEXTURE PASTE **Top and above** Texture paste can be mixed directly with paint. Here, the paste is laid directly onto the bare canvas and then covered with paint to create a strong texture.

thicken the paint so that it holds the marks of the brush or knife used to apply it. A whole range of textures is available with this medium: the thickened paint can be modelled, carved and scratched, and the medium's adhesive properties allow all sorts of foreign bodies to be included in imaginative compositions.

When acrylic is thinned with water and matt medium it can be used rather like egg tempera, with the gradations made up of precise brushstrokes. The addition of matt medium also increases the flow of the paint, making it a little bit thicker. When painting wet into wet the addition of matt medium allows an extra element of precision, since it tends to hold the blurred shape.

Acrylic paints are compatible with other paints and work well in combination with them, which often adds variety to a work. There is one thing to remember, however, which is that although acrylics can be used under oils as an underpainting, they cannot be used on top of oils.

The Hustler

This image was created as one of a set of six postcards, and the composition was determined by using pieces of layout paper. Different elements were drawn on different pieces of paper and then, after a great deal of readjustment, stuck together in the most effective arrangement. The image was transferred to watercolour paper using a light box.

Acrylic thinned heavily with water was flooded over in washes. When this had dried, further washes were added, but where a colour was to remain unaltered glue was painted over the area as a mask. Removing the glue damaged the surface, intentionally, but randomly, thus creating textured, mottled effects. As the painting progressed, thicker paint was used and the surface was scratched into, with dark areas emphasized with charcoal. The lapels of the jacket were made from bits of snakeskin glued to the surface.

Above Colin Williams *The Hustler:* acrylic and collage, 30 × 41 in (76 × 104 cm)

Still Life

This still life was painted directly from the objects, the composition being arrived at "live" rather than pre-organized on paper. It was executed on hardboard primed with household emulsion (water-based paint) applied with a roller, which provides a texture that can be varied according to the amount of paint used and the pressure applied.

Once the drawing was accurately established in pencil, the tones were indicated right across the image in washes of burnt umber. Using acrylic "neat", with no medium or retarder, broad areas of colour were painted in to establish the local colour of the objects. Working from dark to light, tonal adjustments were made using a "dry" technique, which can create rather random effects of scrubbed, rough blending.

Illustrators frequently work to a much larger format than the finished reproduction, and although some physical details are often lost, such variations in paint surface can look very effective.

Under Pressure

Pencil sketches were made to explore the possibilities offered by the subject, and a rough was established. The car was photographed from the appropriate angles, and the figure was photographed separately, care being taken to ensure that it conformed to the perspective of the car and that the figure sat at the height of the running board.

A Grant enlarger (camera lucida) was used to project the photographs onto the board, enabling the artist to reduce or enlarge selected parts of the photographic images. The painting was developed from the background forward, which allowed the artist to obtain clarity of images by overlapping.

In order to achieve the gloss effect on the car, acrylic retarder was added to the paint to allow sensitive blending. Three shades of green were mixed and a separate brush was used for each; the combination of these tones when merged together on the surface produced great variety. The highlights were overlaid as thin washes over the more strongly modelled greens.

Black Hen

The image presented here is essentially an example of paint applied in flat areas; the tube colours were used with only a very little water. A typical passage is the body of the chicken, where the main shape was established in black paint and the feathers painted on. The brushwork is free and unrestrained, the paint being dragged across the surface of the canvas board.

An effect of age was created using a proprietary "crackle varnish" treatment. This entails the use of an oil-based varnish and an acrylic-based varnish .

Left and above Kevin Cunningham (S.)
Still Life: acrylic, 25 × 18½ in
(63 × 47 cm)

Top Kevin Cunningham (S.) *Under
Pressure:* acrylic, 16 × 19 in (40 × 48
cm)

Right Chris Moore (A. P.) *Black Hen:*
acrylic, 19½ × 13½ in (50 × 34 cm)

COLLAGE

Collage is the use of cut paper shapes, printed matter and extraneous items to produce an image of varied texture. First used by Georges Braque (1882–1963) and Pablo Picasso (1881–1973), collage was much favoured by the Dadaists and Surrealists, and in his later years Henri Matisse (1869–1954) preferred this medium to paint.

Photo-collage is the rearrangement of images culled from printed matter such as newspapers and magazines, a re-assembly that creates new forms and meanings.

The Rat

This was an illustration for an article written by an ex-striptease artiste, in which she described pin-striped businessmen, the peep-show voyeurs, as "rats shaking the cubicles they stand in". The magazine seized on the theme of rats and wanted an image that combined a rat's head with a human figure.

The artist developed the idea of two separate environments in one place – one quiet, one menacing – and then set about finding photographic source material. Having discovered suitable images, both from his own collection and in the local library, he used a photocopier to enlarge and reduce them as necessary. After the picture had been assembled and photocopied, grey washes were painted on the print. The texture of the floor where the stripper stands was achieved by using Conté crayon on a rough paper, producing a grainy quality which was further accentuated by the copying process. The photograph of the rat's head was given a quality similar to that of a pen drawing by progressively enlarging the image on the photocopier.

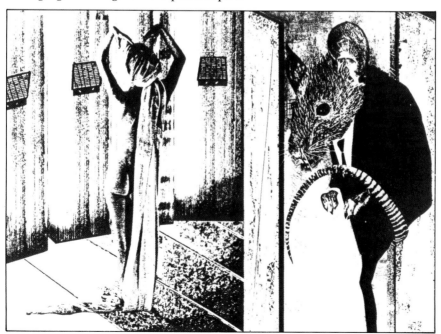

Above left Simon Edwards *Pinkie's Club:* collage, 11½ × 8½ in (30 × 22 cm)

Above right Caroline Grimshaw *Amsterdam:* collage, 11½ × 9½ in (29 × 24 cm)

Left Simon Edwards *The Rat:* collage, 9 × 13 in (23 × 34 cm)

Right David Watson *The Science that Lies in the Soil:* paper-making collage, 11½ × 8½ in (29 × 22 cm)

Oh, here comes the keeper (oppasser!) with a tremendous piece (geweldig stuk!) of horse-meat (paardevlees!). They make dear pets to keep (zijn dure lievelingsdieren om te onderhouden!).

Pinkie's Club

The client asked for an image containing a pair of heavyweight bouncers for the front cover of a magazine which featured an article on local nightclubs.

The faces of the bouncers were assembled from pieces of black and white photographs of faces taken from various magazines; the bodies were also assemblages from various sources. With the figures established, the artist mapped out the rest of the image around them before researching suitable photographs and textures to suit his planned background. The wall came from the artist's own collection of photographs, and the female figure from a book on Winston Churchill, her flapper hat blocked out with opaque white. The source images, being of different sizes, were enlarged or reduced to conform to the scale of the piece.

The individual elements were photocopied first in black and white and then on a colour machine; by adjusting the setting the artist could vary the overall colour of the image – to greenish, brownish, and so on – and thus establish a particular mood or feeling. The sign was contrived by using instant lettering and brushmarks to give a scruffy realism.

The various parts of the picture in their photocopied state were carefully cut around with a scalpel and glued down onto a thin board to form the main artwork.

The repeated copying, enlargement and reduction and adjustment of tone altered the photographic image, often in a chance, random manner. For example, the pavement became more gritty with repeated enlargement. Half-tone dots on printed matter sometimes create a new texture, while at other times they disappear altogether.

The painting itself was done with watercolour, care being taken not to use too much water in case it distorted the board, and the underlying printed tones impart a richness to the colour.

Amsterdam

The artist worked out a rough design and then proceeded to draw on watercolour paper using a 2B pencil, the pencil being continually sharpened in order to give a consistent, intense line. The areas of colour were established using watercolour. Items collected in Amsterdam and culled from Dutch magazines were then stuck down on to the image to add emphasis to it. On the collage thus created further marks were made using pencil, pastel, crayon and opaque white.

The essential quality of this collage is organization of disparate elements – like an irregular jigsaw – into a coherent design.

The Science that Lies in the Soil

This image, used for the over of an edition of *New Scientist* magazine, combined decorative appeal with editorial relevance. The method used, with its organic process, added potency to the image. The basis of this method is paper-making, pulp placed on a mesh screen and allowed to dry. Every shape and area of colour was created by a certain pulp mixture laid in its appropriate place. The layers of sedimentary rock were made of pulp containing relevant matter – rock, shells, gravel; the hedge was formed with a pulp made of grass; the soil of the field was earth pressed into a wet pulp; the trees were fern fronds and the fence made of pieces of wood and wire. The tractor was a metal toy sliced thinly with a hacksaw and pressed into the wet pulp.

This whole collage was allowed to dry and transported carefully to be photographed.

AIRBRUSH

The basic principle of the airbrush is that air under pressure, when passed over paint or ink, atomizes the liquid and creates a fine, even spray. It is the same principle as the mouth-blown atomizer, but a great deal more sophisticated. In the airbrush, compressed air rushes past an outlet from the paint reservoir, creating a vacuum that draws out the fluid. This mixes with the air and travels to the surface of the image in the form of tiny droplets.

The number of airbrushes on the market is vast and bewildering, but there are two basic types. The simplest is the single-action lever mechanism. Here the nature of the spray is varied by altering the distance between the brush and surface. This relative lack of sophistication means that this type is most often used for background work.

The double-action lever airbrush allows more control and variety. The lever controls both the air and the colour. The more you press down, the more air is released; the more you pull back, the more paint is released into the airstream. The compressed air can be supplied by many methods – aerosol can, foot pump, refillable canister, and electric compressor. The last-mentioned is the most expensive and most efficient.

The precise internal workings of the airbrush demand that it be kept clean and maintained in accordance with the manufacturer's recommendations to ensure correct functioning and preserve what is a sizeable investment. To avoid clogging and tainting, the paint reservoir should be cleaned with each change of colour by spraying water or special solvent – whichever is appropriate – through the fluid chamber until clear.

The ideal medium for use with an airbrush is one that sprays finely, does not show the grain of the board, and keeps its colour when sprayed. A quick drying time facilitates rapid work, allowing a mask to be quickly applied to a sprayed area so that a new section of the image can be worked on. Ink, watercolour, gouache and acrylic paint are all commonly used in airbrushes.

The airbrush artist generally uses surfaces with very little texture, since a fibrous surface might lift off and disintegrate with the repeated laying down and removal of masks.

The basic skills include the creation of faultless flat tones, progressions of tone over large areas, brush ruling (sliding the airbrush along an angled straight edge) and curved shapes with soft edges.

The use of masks is an essential part of the airbrush user's repertoire. For accurate and complicated shapes an adhesive masking film is used, and the various sections of the image are cut out with a very sharp scalpel (X-acto knife). A section of the mask is removed and the area sprayed and allowed to dry; that section is then replaced and the process repeated. Clearly, the artist must examine the image carefully and prepare a thoughtful plan of attack so that he or she can make the best possible use of the mask. The mask will, of course, become covered with sprayed colour and will obscure the image underneath, making colour judgement difficult. It can be cleaned with something fine, like cotton buds (swabs), but it is simpler, if more expensive, to use fresh sheets of masking film, and indeed pressure of time may necessitate this.

Liquid mask is used for masking out irregular areas and small parts of the image that need to be protected from spray. It can be removed easily by peeling once the sprayed area has completely dried. Hand-held masks, such as a stencil cut from cardboard, are employed when a soft edge is required.

A special air cap can be fitted to the airbrush to create an irregular spatter effect, which can be used to produce textured tonal changes and unusual backgrounds of mixed colour. A more even spatter can be made by reducing the air pressure.

AIRBRUSHING EFFECTS
To produce fine lines **1** use the edge of a ruler as a guide. For graded tones **2** and blended colours **3** work from light to dark. For a mottled effect **4** a special splatter cap can be fitted to the airbrush.

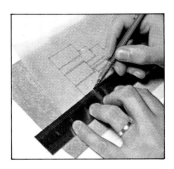

MASKING FILM **1** Trace the image onto the masking film.

2 Cut the masking film with a scalpel, taking care not to score the art surface.

3 Lift one cut mask, spray and allow to dry. Replace the mask and repeat the procedure until the painting is complete.

Musket

Library research into musket mechanisms was developed into a simple, direct diagram using "ghosting" to describe the internal arrangements. In a "ghosted" illustration those elements that would be hidden from view in a solid object are allowed to show through, thus rendering the form transparent.

The line was drawn with a straightedge and templates using a technical pen, the strong line of which provided a positive guide for cutting the mask. A circular template was used to convey the movement of the ball; the template was moved along and the circle re-sprayed over the dry layer of paint.

After the image was airbrushed in watercolour, the grain of the wood was achieved with the use of both sable brushes and water-soluble pencils.

Mask film was used for the solid areas. One area cut and sprayed, the mask replaced, then another area cut, and so on. The sphere was created by careful airbrushing and an eraser was used to describe the final highlight.

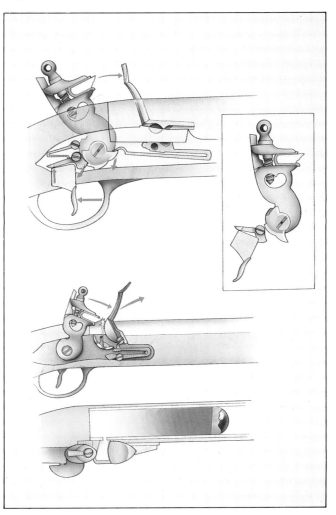

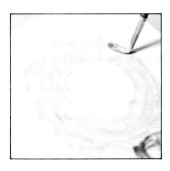

MASKING FLUID **1** Mask the required area with fluid.

2 Spray over the required area and allow to dry.

3 The mask can be removed by careful rubbing and peeling.

Left Jonathan Potter (S.)
Technical painting of a musket:
airbrush, 12 × 8½ in (30 × 22 cm)

Encyclopedia of Aircraft

For this book jacket the art director gave the artist an outline drawing of the layout required and a photograph of the aircraft selected, requesting a very realistic image. Unhappy with the angle of the aircraft in the photographs, the artist purchased a plastic model kit of the aircraft type specified, assembled it as accurately as possible, and took photographic references from a number of viewpoints. Transparencies were also taken of a suitable sky – from a book on aircraft in the artist's extensive source library – to be used as the basis for the background.

Using a slide projector, fixed overhead, he then projected the image of the plane down onto a fine-quality line board, having given due consideration to the overall design and the areas that had to be left free for type. He then carefully drew a pencil outline on the board.

The outline of the aircraft was cut from masking film and the background part removed, leaving the machine covered. Acrylic paint was used to airbrush the sky. The sea was painstakingly hand-painted in acrylic using a meticulous cross-hatching technique, and the clouds were established with the airbrush and the occasional use of a brush for some of the outlines.

A tracing paper mask was cut to cover the background area to within an inch around the aircraft and placed over the background, and the accurately cut masking film was then positioned on top. This was done to prevent the mask film from lifting parts, however tiny, of the completed background painting, which would entail much fiddly repair work.

Several masks were cut from the film to create the basic shapes of the aircraft, and tones were drawn in with the airbrush onto the flat shapes of the underpainting. Soft edges were formed by the use of a handheld mask made of cardboard. The highlight along the fuselage was produced by rubbing off some of the paint with a typewriter eraser, and most of the fine details on the aircraft were hand-painted using a small sable brush.

Right Chris Moore (A. P.), airbrush From left to right *Squash Ball:* 5½ × 5½ in (14 × 14 cm), *Golf Ball:* 7 × 7 in (18 × 18 cm), *Tennis Ball:* 7 × 7 in (18 × 18 cm)

The sky was painted with opaque colour, the aircraft with translucent colour, and the contrast in quality helped to make the main focal point stand out from the backdrop.

Starbridge

This is the kind of image that most people immediately associate with the airbrush. The super-realism that can be created with the medium is an ideal method of realizing the science fiction writer's flights of fancy. The perfect engineering on the grand scale and the crystalline atmosphere can be very precisely described by means of lucid airbrush images.

The broad area of the sky was established first, then the moon was sprayed down, followed by the stars, which were individually drawn with the airbrush. The form of the metallic planet was created with the airbrush and the lines of the surface painted with a brush over pencil guidelines. The spacecraft was carefully masked to define the structure, and coloured pencils were used to add surface colour and texture.

Balls

The ability to describe tonal variation on basic geometric shapes is an essential airbrushing skill. Here are examples of one of those basic shapes, the sphere, being used in the "real world" of commercial illustration.

The squash ball was relatively straightforward, with the dot a hand-painted addition, but the golf ball was a more difficult image to produce, involving as it did the use of a whole variety of ellipse templates in order to create the dimples on the surface. The artist worked from dark to light and then back into the middle tones; the highlights were hand painted.

When the sphere had been established with the airbrush, the hairs of the tennis ball were painted on by hand, and the ball was re-sprayed and then re-painted until the texture was satisfactory.

Above Chris Moore (A. P.) *Starbridge:* airbrush, 14 × 19 in (35 × 48 cm)

Left Chris Moore (A. P.) *Encyclopedia of Aircraft:* airbrush, 13 × 26 in (33 × 66 cm)

PRINTMAKING

RELIEF PRINTING

 In relief printing a block is cut or incised and the portion remaining is inked and printed – it is the negative or non-image areas that are carved away, with the design standing in relief.

WOODCUT

Early examples of this technique date from the 9th century in China, but woodcut illustration in the West was unknown before the 15th century, when it developed in conjunction with printing. This early work took the form of images in pamphlets and books, and was also used for playing cards. In the 16th century woodcut illustration declined and engraving on copper became the most widely used method, but towards the end of the 19th century it received new impetus, partly from the import of the Japanese prints.

Albrecht Dürer *Artist using a grid for measured drawing* (detail): woodcut.

The wood used for woodcuts is cut with the grain. Modern artists have exploited the grain of the softwoods to create visual effects, whereas the Old Masters, in their pursuit of detail, preferred fine grains. Various tools are employed to make the different cuts. Knives, held upright, are used for fine work and outlines, while gouges are used to clear away the unwanted wood around the image. Chisels and gouges of all sizes are used to create pattern and texture on the surface area.

The ink, which is applied to the surface of the block by means of a roller, is sufficiently sticky not to flow into the small detailed areas. Coloured prints can be achieved by various means, but usually they are produced by cutting separate blocks for each colour, which are then printed in sequence. Great care must be taken to register the blocks accurately. Alternatively, when a print has been taken of the whole image, part of the design can be eliminated and the block inked up in

MAKING A WOODCUT

WOODCUT **1** Wash the block with white paint to make a clear base for the traced drawing.

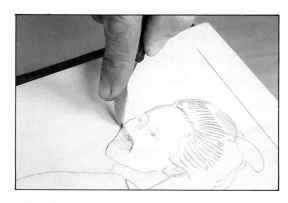

2 Use a sharp knife to cut outlines. To remove a fine furrow of wood, cut around the outline again with the knife blade angled slightly to the first cut.

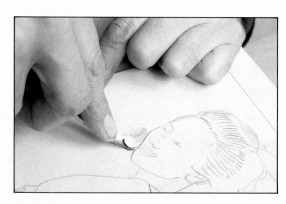

3 Use a gouge to remove large areas of wood, working into the incised outline for a clean shape. Use a V-shaped tool to work fine lines and small details.

another colour and printed over the first print; this can be repeated until a considerable range of colour has been achieved. Another procedure is to cut up the finished woodcut like a jigsaw puzzle and ink each piece separately. It is then reassembled to produce the final print. The Japanese favoured painting the colours on the block before each print.

Oil-based inks have an advantage over water-based inks when the artist is making a series of prints, since they remain usable over a long period, whereas water-based inks tend to dry on the slab.

The bold contrast of black and white is particularly useful when the image is to be printed on cheaper papers, as their porous nature can often obscure subtle tonal differences.

Left Jane Smith *Candide and the Minister:* woodcut, 14 × 5½ in (36 × 14 cm)

Below left Jane Smith *Candide and Cunégonde:* woodcut, 11½ × 7 in (29 × 18 cm)

Candide and the Minister

The colours of this image were established at different stages of the process.

The main shapes of the house, tree and figures were cut and the whole surface of the block inked up with the lighter of the browns. Small patches of other colours were dabbed on certain areas – for example, green on the tree and red on the figure. The block was then printed. Those areas which were to remain light brown in the finished print were eliminated, and the areas remaining were inked up with dark brown. At this stage blue was added to the figure in the foreground. The printing of the amended block on the first print produced the final image.

Candide and Cunegonde

The essential characteristics of the woodcut image are clearly shown in this example of a woodcut illustration. The obligation to cut with the grain has dictated the design to some extent. The grass points in the direction of the grain, and the tracery of the branches was influenced by the structure of the wood. The presence of the grain, however, provides visual interest in the solid areas, appearing as white, running flecks.

The line which runs across the image – and across the grain – had to be treated with care. The knife was angled to avoid undercutting the surface of the wood, as such an undercut would collapse under the pressure of printing. The majority of cuts were made with gouges of various shapes and sizes, while some of the very fine incisions were made with a scalpel (X-acto knife).

LINOCUT

Linoleum can be used instead of wood to produce images that have many of the visual qualities of wood-cuts. When linoleum is warmed, it is much easier to cut and gouge than wood; and, of course, it has no grain to dictate the direction of the cut.

Above A piece of linoleum has been cut and inked up **left.** The lighter areas are the uncut, relief surfaces which print dark **right**.

TAKING A PRINT **1** Ink the roller on a pad impregnated with oil-based inks.

2 Roll the ink evenly over the surface of the block.

3 Place a sheet of paper on the block and rub with a baren, or any smooth rounded object.

4 Carefully remove the paper from the block and allow the ink to dry.

Feet

This particularly bold image is typical of the freedom provided by the linocut technique, which allows curved marks to be made in a bold, decisive fashion. The accurate line was carved using a fine V-tool, while the larger areas of white were cleared away with a U-shaped gouge.

The print was made on typing paper, which responds very well to detail.

Above Jane Smith *Feet:* linocut, 4 × 4 in (10 × 10 cm)

Rice and Beads

This is an example of a relief print, which is produced by using separate blocks inked up individually. These are positioned together and printed as one image onto textured paper, a process that allows precise demarcation of colours.

Buskers

Monoprints are created by applying oil-based inks to a glass slab, onto which paper is pressed, often achieving random and various effects.

Patterns can be created by texturing the ink surface – with a finger, brushes, or drops of turpentine – and the dried print can be further textured by rubbing over it with sandpaper. Photocopying can alter it still further.

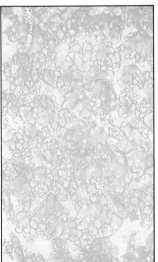

Above left Jane Smith *Rice and Beads:* linocut, 5 × 4 in (13 × 10 cm)

Above right Jane Smith *Buskers:* linocut, 15 × 12 in (38 × 30 cm)

Far left and left Two examples of Jane Smith's collection of monoprints which she uses as backgrounds for many of her prints.

The initial choice of paper is important, as it considerably affects the outcome. This artist has built up a source bank of multi-coloured and multi-textured paper which she can use as backgrounds for her linocuts and prints.

The variety within the single impression of the linocut was achieved by rolling the lightest colour over the lino image and by dabbing on different colours in various places – sometimes on their own, sometimes as a mixture with the main colour. Random effects were created as the ink met the varied surfaces and colours presented by the monoprint collage. The image was completed by the addition of specific pieces of tissue paper and some crayon marks.

WOOD ENGRAVING

In wood engraving an end-grain of wood is used, and the blocks are characteristically smaller and the engravings more intricate. Generally the whites – the cuts – are the positive image on a black background. The wood engraving technique was developed to its height in the 18th century with the artist, Thomas Bewick (1753–1828), creating "colour" with a vast range of tones and texture in his sensitive pastoral scenes. During the 19th century the technique was used as a way of reproducing artists' drawings and illustrations, but it was largely superseded by developments in printing processes and, in particular, the invention of photo-mechanical methods. The private presses in the 1920s and 1930s used engravers, and such people as Eric Gill

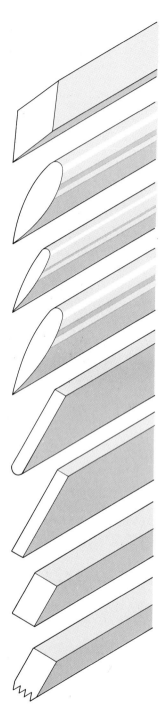

Above Wood engraving tools From top to bottom, a gravure or lozenge, a spitstick, two tint tools, a round scauper, a square scauper, a chisel and a multi-tint tool.

Right Thomas Bewick *Waiting for Death* This wood engraving, Bewick's last work, was left unfinished.

(1882–1940) and Eric Ravilious (1903–1942) produced fine examples of the craft.

The main tool is the graver, which has a diamond cross-section at an angle to the shaft; the thicker the blade the thicker the line. Variety is achieved by altering the angle of approach to the surface and by subtle changes of pressure. The convex or elliptical cross-section of the spitsticker facilitate the production of curved lines; the scorper is used for clearing small areas and cutting broad lines. Triangular tools used with great precision produce "tints" by means of regular and graded parallel lines; multiple tools are designed to produce an incision of precise parallel lines.

Such a demanding medium requires planning. Before cutting, the artist can indicate the image in a soft pencil, which does not mark the surface, or in fountain pen ink, the dyes of which penetrate the wood. A coating of ink – black or coloured – allows the cuts to be seen clearly as they are made. Apart from wood, perspex (Lucite) and linoleum are among the materials that have been widely used for this technique.

Oil-based ink is the type most commonly used, with the usual variable being the type of paper used, with different textures and absorbencies dictating, to a large extent, the definition and surface quality of the finished engraving. The paper is placed on the inked block and rubbed on the back with a burnisher, which can be anything smooth, from a spoon to a tool specifically used for this purpose in etching. Usually the paper is protected by a thin piece of cardboard, which receives the direct pressure. Colour prints can be achieved with the use of multiple blocks.

ENGRAVING A WOOD BLOCK
1 Using a sandbag as a support to the wood block, always cut curves by rotating the block, not the tool.

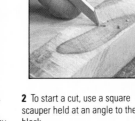

2 To start a cut, use a square scauper held at an angle to the wood block.

3 Once an incision has been made, lower the scauper and continue to cut at a shallow angle.

4 Use a lozenge-shaped tool to cut fine, straight lines.

PROOFING A WOOD ENGRAVING
1 Ink up the block in a dark colour and cover with a sheet of paper. Rub the surface with a smooth, rounded object.

5 Use spitsticks to 'draw' on the block.

2 Remove the paper and allow the proof to dry thoroughly.

3 If an area of the proof appears too solid and dark, return to the block and make a series of parallel cuts with a small spitstick.

Sky

In this illustration, one of a series of atmospheric images, the artist manipulated the black and white, linear medium to create a range of tones.

She took the image from a charcoal drawing, but did not attempt to copy it, preferring to use the tonal variation it displayed as a starting point. A brief indication of the outline of the cloud was drawn in ink on a stained background, and the cuts were made across the whole image in preference to working a single area to completion. Proofs were taken at regular intervals, thus giving the artist a clear indication of the progress in terms of black and white; this was particularly necessary in such a tonal piece.

The image was, in essence, built up in layers. Some tones were built up as a line pattern using a graver to

make parallel strokes and tapered marks; others, of a softer nature, were created using multiple tool marks in curved overlaps and more angular arrangements. Into these "greys" white was added using wider tools. The black areas were given a "sparkle" with tiny, fine marks cut into the surface.

Dockside

The artist explored the potential of the subject – the brickwork, for example – in a preliminary drawing, and then put a quite detailed drawing, indicating the shape of the building and the types of window, on the block, emphasizing the pattern.

The characteristic quality of this image is the intricate arrangement of very fine lines made with a graver. The large areas of white were cleared away using broad tools including the chisel, which produced a very clean-edged mark.

Landscape

Drawings and photographs were used as reference for this image. An outline drawing was first established. The shadow on the foreground tree was then painted on as a solid area of ink in order to maintain its pres-

ence during the engraving process. In the initial stages the artist concentrated on the texture and shape of the tree, creating these effects with regular cuts with the graver.

Both the perfect wood surface and the perfect black it produces when printed were exploited in this image, with something like half the area of the block being left uncut. The light flecks on the dark area were made by lightly touching the wood with the sharp tool.

Far left Clare Hemstock (S.) *Sky:* wood
engraving, 2 × 4 in (5 × 10 cm)

Left Clare Hemstock (S.) *Dockside:* wood
engraving, 2½ × 2½ in (6 × 6 cm)

Below left Clare Hemstock (S.)
Landscape: wood engraving, 3 × 5 in
(8 × 13 cm)

Below right Clare Hemstock
(S.) *Pimp, Tethora and Sethora:* wood
engravings, 2 × 3 in (5 × 8 cm); 2 ×
1½ in (5 × 4 cm); 2 × 2 in (5 × 5 cm)

Pimp, Tethora and Sethora

Here we see three images from a book on the sheep
numbering system used by shepherds to count their
sheep. The initial drawings captured the character of
the different animals, and for the image of *Pimp,* a
Lincoln Longwool, Clare Hemstock used a wide range
of tools and marks in order to describe the very woolly
animal. Similar shapes of graver line were varied by
using different pressures, and blobs of white were
created by sticking the graver straight into the wood
and turning it round – the greater the pressure, the
larger the circle.

Working on such small blocks made the artist aware
of the importance of each mark she made, and it is, of
course, the nature of the medium that mistakes cannot
be corrected.

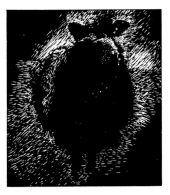

INTAGLIO PRINTING

In intaglio printing the positive image is cut below the surface of the block or plate and it is this line that carries the ink that produces the print. Both engraving and etching have made significant contributions to the history of illustration, but the processes are so time-consuming that they are rarely used by the modern illustrator.

ENGRAVING

Scratched images have a history that dates back to pre-historic man, and throughout the years engraving has been used for surface decoration on ornamental and functional objects. Prints from engraved surfaces first appeared in the 15th century. In Germany Martin Schongauer (d 1491) worked with delicate shading, reflecting the naturalism of Gothic art, whereas the more aesthetic concerns of the Italians produced such pieces as the famous *Battle of the Nudes* by Antonio Pollaiuolo (c 1432–98). By the 17th century highly sophisticated techniques had been developed which enabled engraving to be used for book illustration, reproduction of oil paintings and portraiture. The 19th century saw its replacement as a commercial medium by wood-engraving and later by photo-mechanical methods.

ENGRAVING THE PLATE
1 Rest the plate on a sandbag so that the plate can be freely turned when cutting a curved line.

2 Use a burin, held at a shallow angle, to cut a straight line. Push the blade gently, guiding it with the forefinger.

3 Carefully remove burrs of waste metal with a scraper.

4 Remove unwanted marks by rubbing the area with a burnisher.

The chief tool used is the steel burin, which has a square- or diamond-shaped head, the cutting angle of which is pushed into the metal plate. The deeper the cut, the wider the line, and great variation can be obtained in this way. The burin is available in a variety of widths, and a range of multiple tools exist which produce parallel lines by means of many small cutting points.

The image is drawn directly on the plate using a wax crayon, a felt-tip pen or Indian ink. Copper is the traditionally used surface, though zinc and perspex (Lucite) have also been employed. The essence of the technique is that the hand and the tool remain steady, and changes in direction of line are obtained by manoeuvring the plate with the other hand.

Tone and texture are created by the production of regular parallel lines, arrangements of broken line, and variety of dot types. A burr is produced on either side of the engraved line, and this ridge of metal has to be removed with a scraper in order not to affect the printing. A burnisher is used to erase unwanted marks on the surface of the plate.

Left   Robert Nanteuil *Portrait of Michael le Tellier:* intaglio engraving

9

Above William Blake This illustration is an example of a process Blake termed 'illuminated printing'. The text and design were etched in relief, printed in one colour and then hand tinted.

ETCHING

Etching entails dissolving the surface of a metal plate in a controlled fashion to produce a line that takes the ink. It was originally developed as a quicker method than engraving, but then artists discovered that the greater range of line allowed more freedom of image-making. Experiments had started in the 16th century, and Rembrandt (1606–69) was an exponent of the draughtsman-like qualities of the medium. In the 18th century the tonal methods of aquatint and soft ground were developed and used to advantage in the works of, among others, William Hogarth (1697–1764), Thomas Rowlandson (1756–1827) and James Gillray (1757–1815). William Blake (1757–1827) invented a relief process in which both the text and the illustration were printed at the same time, but generally etching was overtaken by the new developments in printing in the 19th century and declined as a medium for illustration.

The plate – copper or zinc – is thoroughly degreased, and a bitumen and wax ground is applied. The design is scratched into this coating, exposing the metal underneath; but care must be taken not to damage the surface. The plate is then immersed in acid; the longer it stays in, the deeper the etched line will be, and in consequence the darker the printed line. Variety can be achieved by subjecting selected lines to reduced or extended periods. With the aid of an acid-resistant varnish, revealed areas of the plate requiring less exposure can be protected from the process, while the deeper lines are being etched.

The plate is cleaned with solvent and thick black ink is applied. The surface is then wiped clean, leaving ink only in the bitten line. Damp paper is laid over the plate and the two passed, under great pressure, through the

HARD GROUND ETCHING
1 Warm a degreased plate and dab with a ball of hard ground.

2 Spread the ground over the plate with a roller.

3 Smooth out the coating by drawing the roller across the plate in one direction.

4 Clamp the plate upside down over lighted tapers. Move the tapers until the whole surface blackens.

5 Draw into the waxy coating with an etching needle, taking care not to scratch the surface of the plate.

6 Paint out any flaws in the coating and coat the edges of the plate with stop-out varnish to prevent foul biting.

ETCHING THE PLATE
1 When the stop-out varnish has dried, lower the plate into the acid bath with a loop of string.

2 During the etching process, remove any bubbles from the surface of the plate with a wooden-handled brush or a feather.

3 After the required time, remove the plate carefully and rinse under running water.

rollers of an intaglio press. The process can be repeated and adjustments made to the surface between each proof.

Uniform tone is achieved by the aquatint process. An even coating of resin is dusted onto the plate, which is then heated so that the resin fuses with the metal. When the plate has cooled, the negative of the design is painted out using acid-resistant varnish. When immersed in acid, the metal lying between the molten particles of resin is attacked and a fine texture is produced. The longer the plate is in the acid the darker the tone produced when printed; the ink settles in the bitten areas while the metal protected by the resin prints as minute white dots. Scraping and burnishing an aquatint will produce fine tonal gradations.

A soft ground – made of bitumen and wax mixed with Vaseline – is one that does not harden when rolled on the plate. A piece of thin paper is placed on the ground and a pencil drawing made on it; when the paper is removed the ground lifts away where the pencil point exerted pressure. The variable, broken, line has the appearance of chalk or soft pencil when etched and printed. All sorts of textures and materials – from feathers to metal mesh – can be pressed into a soft ground to provide variety in the print.

Sugar aquatint allows the production of positive brush marks on an etching. A solution of sugar, soap and Indian ink is used to paint the design on the plate, which is then covered with a hard ground. The plate is immersed in warm water and the sugar dissolves, lifting off the hard ground and exposing the bare metal. The painted shapes can be given texture either with a soft ground or with an aquatint.

For dry-point, a very sharp needle, either made of hard steel or tipped with a hard stone, is used. As the point runs across the surface of the plate, a ridge, or burr, of metal is thrown up on either side of the line. It is this burr that retains the ink, giving the print its dis-

AQUATINTING
1 On a prepared plate, use stop-out varnish to paint out the areas to appear white in the final print. Varnish the edges and back of the print and immerse in acid for about 15 seconds.

2 Rinse the plate and blot dry. Stop out the light grey tones and again immerse the plate in acid for a shorter period of time.

3 Repeat the process until the required number of tones are bitten into the plate.

4 Finally, remove the stop-out varnish with white spirit and the rosin with methylated spirits and proof the plate.

TAKING AN INTAGLIO PRINT
1 Soak the paper in clean water. (The period of time varies according to the type of paper.)

5 Use tissue to complete the cleaning process.

9 Cover the plate and paper with blankets.

2 File the edges of the plate with a burnishing tool, held at an angle.

6 Polish the plate with the side of the hand, lightly dusted with French chalk.

10 Roll the print through the press, making sure that no creases form in the blankets.

3 Warm the plate and work a thick coating of ink into the intaglio, using a circular motion.

7 Blot the soaked paper.

11 Remove the blankets and carefully peel away the print.

4 Wipe the surface of the plate with muslin to clear away residual ink.

8 Place the plate on the bed of the press and cover with the paper.

12 Check the print. An ill-defined print will be caused by using too dry ink or over-wet paper.

SOFT GROUND ETCHING
1 Prepare the plate with soft ground, lay it on the bed of the press and arrange with textured objects. Cover with greaseproof paper and run through the press.

2 Carefully remove the blankets, greaseproof paper and objects. Stop out the blank areas of the plate and etch in acid.

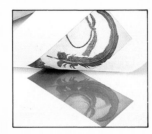

3 Clean the plate with white spirit and proof.

tinctive soft quality. The ridge of metal is quickly worn down by the pressure of the press and can be used only for a limited number of prints. Dry-point is often used to reinforce etchings, being worked on the part of the plate that needs to be darkened; Rembrandt frequently used the technique in this way.

London Walk

This composite image involved the use of photographic material, and hence a more complicated etching process. The printed element of the image was enlarged to the required size and put onto film. The cleaned plate was coated with a light-sensitive solution, known as photo resist. The transparent positive was laid on the plate, exposed to ultra-violet light, and then placed in a dish of resist developer. The developer washed away the lines and dots, the part of the image that appeared opaque on the positive film, while the remaining area stayed covered with the light-hardened solution, which is acid resistant.

A proof was made of this first stage, and a standard ground was applied to the plate drawn into with an etching needle. The drawing was built up in several stages, and a proof was taken at each stage. As a final adjustment the artist burnished some of the lines – for example, the small squares which appear to fade gradually.

The final prints were made using black ink for the etched areas, and coloured inks were dabbed on using little pads of gauze. When the prints had dried watercolour washes were added.

Waste Paper

This image, which developed from studies of the contents of a waste-paper basket, also involved photographic elements, which were put on to the plate first. The line drawing was done using a range of mark widths and a variety of immersion times. A soft ground was put on the plate and lace pressed into it; when removed, this left a subtle pattern where the metal was exposed to the effect of the acid.

The final prints were made using brown and blue inks and, when they were dry, items from the waste bin were stuck on. Watercolour was used to add splashes of colour.

As We Forgive

The art director responsible for finding a suitable image for this book chanced upon this etching in the artist's portfolio and saw its potential.

Right Caroline Grimshaw *Waste Paper:* intaglio etching, 5 × 4 in (13 × 10 cm)

Above left and right Gino D'Achille *As We Forgive:* intaglio etching, 11½ × 14½ in (29 × 37 cm) A print of the etching **left** was hand painted in watercolour **right**.

Far left Caroline Grimshaw *London Walk:* intaglio etching, 3 × 3 in (7.5 × 7.5 cm)

The image was established using a soft ground, with the artist drawing directly on paper laid over the ground, which produced the charcoal-like quality to the illustration. The textures were made using a variety of materials, and specific details, such as the features of the face, were defined and accentuated using the dry-point technique. The general range of tones was created by progressive subjection to the acid, the intense areas of blue being built up with a dry-point needle.

The art director reduced the etching to the required size and made a photographic reproduction on a fine-quality art paper. This is capable of accepting water-colour; it was stretched, and loose washes of thin watercolour applied over the image.

LITHOGRAPHY

Unlike engraving and etching, lithography is a planographic process; that is, the print is made directly from the surface of the plate or stone. The process, unlike relief or intaglio print-making, does not necessitate the use of tools; it is basically a drawing method, and allows the artist to work directly and with some freedom. The process was invented by Alois Senefelder in 1797, and was originally used for delicate tonal work. In the course of the 19th century its expressive possibilities were fully explored by artists such as Henri de Toulouse-Lautrec (1864–1901); and since this time it has been extremely popular with artists.

The process is based on the mutual antipathy of water and grease. The surface – a lithographic stone or specially grained zinc or aluminium plate – is thoroughly cleaned and degreased and the positive image is established by drawing or painting with litho crayon or litho ink, both of which are essentially greasy. Litho crayons come in a variety of grades, from very soft to hard, and can produce both extremely subtle gradations of tone as well as dynamic lines. The ink, which comes in stick form, is gently melted over heat and then diluted with water or turpentine. It can be used quite thick for brush work or very fluid for pen drawing. A wide range of textures can be created by, among other things, the use of a sponge and ink spattered from a stiff brush.

When complete, the image is covered with resin and chalk, and the whole surface is treated with a solution of gum arabic, which fixes the grease and ensures that the negative areas are sealed and thus cannot be affected by accidental contact with grease. The ink used to draw the design is cleaned off with turpentine and the excess gum washed off with water, but the grain of the stone or plate retains the grease, and the water will run off the drawn image.

To print, ink is rolled over the plate or stone while it is still damp, so that the printing ink adheres only to the grease image. Proofs can be taken until it is obvious that the image is clogged with ink, when it must be cleaned and re-treated. It is an attractive process but a lengthy one, and thus does not always lend itself to the quickly made images so frequently required of the illustrator.

Coloured lithographs are produced by using several plates or stones, one for each colour, and careful tracing of the design and accurate registration are essential.

Barber Shop

The figure was established on the plate using a litho crayon and then protected with a coating of gum. To make the white marks, gum was dragged on with a brush and spattered off the bristles of a toothbrush. Inks of differing consistency were then painted on top to produce a variety of marks.

1 Draw on the lithographic surface with litho crayons, as if using ordinary pastels or chalks.

2 Waxy pencils can be used for drawing fine lines.

SCREENPRINTING

Screenprinting is a sophisticated version of stencilling. It can be a very simple process, but developments in this century have opened up many technical possibilities, some of which are quite complex. A fine mesh of a special tough but thin fabric is stretched over a strong frame, and the image is made either by glueing a stencil to the screen or by drawing directly on it with litho ink or some other blocking medium. To print, ink is squeezed through the open areas of the mesh using a squeegee – a broad rubber blade held in a wooden handle, and the paper will take the print of the unblocked areas of the screen.

Left Henri de Toulouse-Lautrec *Aux Ambassadeurs:* lithograph. This poster design reveals Lautrec's typical use of simplified line and strong, flat colour.

Below Kevin Cunningham (S.) *Barber Shop:* lithograph, 18 × 15 in (46 × 38 cm)

MAKING A SCREENPRINT
1 Place the stencil film over the design and cut through the top layer with a scalpel.

2 A screen is then laid over the film and wiped with a damp sponge to adhere the film to the mesh.

3 Allow the stencil film to dry, then carefully peel away its acetate backing.

4 Position paper under the screen and pour printing ink onto the edge of the screen.

6 Raise the screen to remove the print. Repeat the process for successive prints.

5 Use a squeegee to draw the ink evenly over the screen, forcing the ink through to the paper.

There are many different ways of putting images on the screen, one of which is to use a film stencil – transparent coloured film on a backing sheet. The image is cut from the film with a knife and peeled away from the backing sheet. The stencil is then placed film side down and attached to the screen using either a solvent or heat, and the backing pulled away.

A lithographic type of image – that is, a positive drawn image – can be achieved by using a solid litho crayon. The drawing is made directly on the screen and then covered with a glue, such as gum arabic. The design is then washed out with turpentine, leaving the glue in the negative areas to act as the stencil.

A positive mask can be cut – that is those areas not to be printed are removed – for use with photo-sensitive gelatin sheets. The cut stencil is placed over the sensitized sheet and the whole assembly exposed to ultraviolet light. The sheet is put into a chemical bath where the areas exposed to light harden; those areas of the gelatin which have not hardened – the positive parts of the design – are washed away with hot water. Photographically produced positives can be used in this way.

INDIRECT PHOTO STENCIL
1 Position the positive film onto the exposure screen, emulsion side up, cover with sensitized gelatin and expose the film to ultraviolet light.

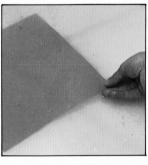

2 Place the gelatin film in a bath containing a solution of 4 parts water to 1 part hydrogen peroxide. Leave for 30 seconds to harden the gelatin.

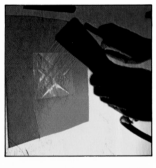

3 Wash the film with water (38°C/111°F). The unexposed gelatin washes away leaving the image clearly visible.

4 Position the gelatin face down onto the printing face of the screen.

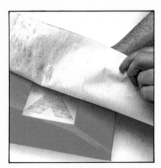

5 Remove residual water from the stencil by blotting with newsprint.

6 Turn the screen over and cover with newsprint. Work over the surface with a roller, forcing the fabric onto the stencil and drawing the gelatin up into the mesh.

7 Allow the stencil to dry, then remove the backing sheet. The image remains on the screen mesh.

Fish

The image was painted on the fine mesh of the screen using litho ink, then a gum resist was put over the whole screen and the image washed out. This was done for each element of the design, and thus required four screens.

In order to obtain a "watercolour" appearance the inks were diluted with extender and printed in the order, yellow, orange, pale blue, and dark blue.

Tube Journey

The artist took her own photographic reference, and made a collage of the chosen images. The collage was then photographed, the image transferred to a fine screen using photo-sensitive gel, and prints were taken using blue ink. The positioning of the two subsequent images was established by laying tracing paper over the original collage and arranging the selected fragments of lettering and photographs upon it. The two compositions were then photographed and put on separate screens. These, one yellow and one red, were carefully registered and printed on the blue image.

The Tiger

The original painting was put on a light box and the areas of colour were carefully traced as blocks of black paint on two overlays – one for the yellow, one for the red.

Photographic positives were made of the three black images and each one put on a separate screen. Printing was done rapidly in order to maintain the grainy quality of the outline.

Above Jane Mitchell (S.)
Fish: screenprint, 3½ × 5 in (9 × 13 cm)

Left Caroline Grimshaw
Tube Journey: screenprint, 9½ × 4 in (24 × 10 cm)

Right Jane Mitchell (S.)
Tiger: screenprint, 6 × 8 in (15 × 20 cm)

SPECIFIC APPLICATIONS

EDITORIAL

In newspapers and magazines, illustrations are often used to amplify the text. The images sometimes relate strictly to the text, are sometimes purely decorative, and sometimes a mixture of both.

![Pigs photo collage](Above Simon Edwards Pigs)

Above Simon Edwards *Pigs:* photo collage, 10½ × 7 in (26.5 × 18.5 cm)

Pigs

This illustration was made to accompany an article in a car magazine describing the freeloading lifestyles of journalists, particularly at car launches where inducements are numerous. The article was a harsh one, and the art director wanted the extra emphasis provided by the image of the pigs; beyond that requirement the artist was given a free rein.

The figures and pig heads were black and white photocopies of photographs, and the background was made of textured and coloured paper. The table laden with food was a collage of separate coloured items taken from the artist's collection of photographs. The total image was assembled and copied using a colour machine, which gave the coloured elements a slightly different quality.

Watercolour was used on the photocopy to heighten and define the black and white parts of the image, for example the features of the pigs and their clothing. The smoke was created from a combination of white paint and white paper.

Avocado

The artist was given a copy of an article to read on natural beauty products and provided images that were to be dropped in on the page, breaking up the copy in an informative and decorative fashion. To establish their presence on the page he chose a technique that produced a strong image, one that had the organic quality of a woodcut print, which suited the text. This was done by making a drawing on watercolour paper and then putting a latex mask over the whole image except for those parts that were to appear black. The image area was then covered with black ink, and when it had dried the mask was removed, revealing the untouched white paper. The colour was added afterwards with watercolours.

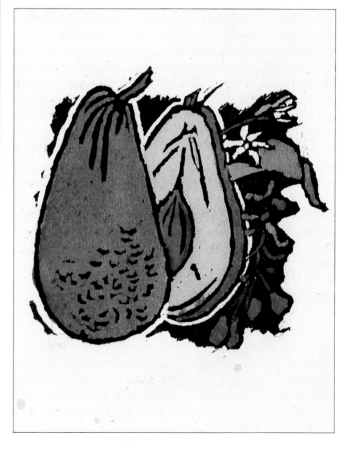

Above David Watson *Avocado:* pen and ink, 2¾ × 2¼ in (7 × 5.5 cm)

GOOD NEWS

LACE AND FAVOUR

You may have already come across the pretty cotton lace panels, bedspreads and tablecloths offered mail order by Anna's Choice. If you love the songbirds, swags of flowers and ribbons, which are all taken from old designs, you'll be delighted to learn that they are now available retail in a new shop and trade showroom which has opened under the name of Anna French. Lace begins at £7.40 a metre and is displayed alongside cotton fabrics from £12.20 a metre and wallpapers from £10.30 a roll. Anna French, 343 King's Rd, London SW3. MB

Illustration/Susan Robertson

OPEN HC

Professional interior designers often have the pick of home furnishings. It's good, therefore, to hear of a designer 'going public'. Ann Chiswell hand-paints and stencils pure cotton or Chinese silk cushion covers. Her new Flowerbasket range has five designs: Roses (illustrated left), Hydrangeas, Peonies, Daisies and Geraniums. She's also launched her first tablelinen collection which includes the fabric Bows and Spots. Available to order in any colourway – minimum 25m – it costs from £8 per metre. Ring 01–992 0196 for stockists. JS

Above and left Susan Robertson (D. W. D.) *Lace and Favour:* pencil, 3¼ × 3½ in (8 × 9 cm)

Lace and Favour

Commissioned to do an illustration for an article called "Lace and Favour", the artist was supplied with a photograph of the bed, together with a sample of the lace and a cushion. She was also given the layout into which her image had to fit and the copy to which the image had to relate.

A preparatory drawing made to determine the composition was then transferred to a good-quality cartridge (drawing) paper and finely drawn with a variety of sharp-pointed pencils.

Below Jane Smith *Leo the Lion:* scraperboard

Leo the Lion

The brief here was open in terms of the treatment of the subject, the only specific requirements being very rigid stipulations with regard to size. The artist was given the width of the space that was to be free down the page and told to fill it in what ever way she pleased with single or repeated images. In fact she produced two pieces of artwork, which the designer of the magazine arranged.

The artist's original conception was visualized in black and white, and so she decided to work on scraperboard. Only when the image had been completed was a colour treatment considered – as an overlay. The acetate was carefully registered and the area of colour painted on with black ink. When supplying the artwork the artist specified the Pantone number for the orange in which the overlay was to be printed.

Above Debbie Hinks (A. P.) *The Plan:* pastel, 30 × 20 in (76 × 51 cm)

The Plan

The brief was to show a woman contemplating the state of her lovelife before going out for the evening with her boyfriend and his other woman friend. The artist chose to illustrate this moment by depicting the woman pausing, in the middle of dressing, to review her situation. The drawing of the figure was done from life, which gave a fresh immediacy well suited to the medium.

When the illustration was presented to the client some changes were requested in the background and in the position of the left knee. The artist cut out a white paper mask, stuck it over the offending area and reworked the design.

Poor, Dear Charlotte

The task here was to produce a series of illustrations to accompany the weekly instalments of a serialized story about a woman who changes her lifestyle dramatically. The artist was given a synopsis of the story, a list of characters, and an indication of who should appear each week. Having read the story and discovered how the characters were described and what clothes they normally wore, the artist took photographs of specially

Above Debbie Hinks (A. P.) *Poor, Dear Charlotte:* pastel, 32 × 23 in (81 × 58.5 cm)

posed models for reference and then produced visualizations, which were presented to the client for approval.

In order to launch the story, the full-colour illustration reproduced above had to act as an indicator of the story line, featuring the main character before and after her transformation. The artist was given free rein to establish the contrast between the old character – a reserved teacher – and the new one – a confident woman of the world.

For the soft skin tones the artist scraped the side of her pastels with a scalpel and applied the fine powder to the paper using cotton wool (absorbent cotton), rubbing it in further with a torchon (stump). The work was then fixed and more fine layers were dabbed on. The rest of the piece was built up using the full range of pastel marks, resulting in a striking image.

Above Biz Hull (A. P.) *Miss Bede is Staying:* coloured pencil, 12 × 19½ in (30.5 × 49.5 cm)

Overcoat

Illustrations are often required for the fashion pages of magazines, as in these examples. The items of clothing were supplied by the magazine and the artist took the photographic reference herself. The first drawing submitted was rejected as being too "human" so the artist elongated the figure in the second version.

It was important to show the details of the garment to advantage – the colours, the trimmings, and so on – however broad the treatment. Coloured pastel described the colour of the printed patterns and the image was completed by the addition of decorative pastel elements which emphasized the sense of movement. Although quite small images when printed, the actual artworks were pastel drawings on 16 × 23 in (40 × 58 cm) paper.

Miss Bede is Staying

This was a demanding brief, since the costumes, carriage and background details had to be strictly in period, and the image had to feature particular characters. The amount of bleed and the area to be left free for copy were also specified.

The photographic reference was projected onto layout paper, and the elements arranged into the desired composition, after which the whole image was transferred onto the final surface and an outline established.

The colours of the drawing were then built up, starting with the faces. Once the surface had been covered with colour, the artist began to establish a balance and to emphasize elements such as the figures – the focal point of the illustration.

Dress

The pose, which was based on a photograph in a magazine devoted to dance, was one that the artist considered ideal for the dress to be illustrated. The intention was to convey an accurate indication of the clothing, but in a dynamic and unfussy manner. The dancer's slimness, emphasized by exaggerating the length of the legs, was used to accentuate the elegance of the garment.

A charcoal pencil drawing was blocked in with flowing Indian ink, and grey and white pastels were used to indicate the softness and delicacy of the chiffon fabric and to highlight the simple facial details. The calligraphic marks of ink painting are particularly well-suited to the task of creating a sense of movement.

Far left Debbie Hinks (A. P.) *Overcoat:* pastel, 30 × 22 in (76 × 56 cm)
Left Debbie Hinks (A. P.) *Dress:* ink and pastel, 30 × 20 in (76 × 51 cm)

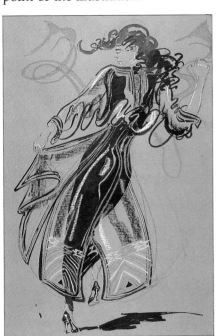

ADVERTISING

ADVERTISING

Advertising is a lucrative and very varied area of work for the illustrator. The fact that a great deal of money may be spent on the total campaign means that the brief issued by the advertising agency is very precise and often involves the illustrator in a meeting with the client.

Hitachi

The requirements of the art director for this advertisement were very specific; the artist was given a visualization in marker pen which indicated the areas taken up with type and told to fit his image around them. He then photographed the objects separately and projected them onto the board.

The forms of the equipment were established, and carefully worked out masks were cut so that the sharply printed graphics could be reproduced precisely. The rounded edge formed by the curved junction of the front with the side was airbrushed in using a piece of cardboard held away from the surface. Ellipse templates were used for the highlights on the buttons.

In order to achieve accuracy in the lettering, the image was projected onto the illustration and the letters painted on by hand.

Akai

This was an advertisement for a new range of modular special-effects recording machines which could be stacked. It was this facility, together with an indication of the machines' performance, that the advertising agency wanted emphasized, and some reference had to be made to the fact that recorded effects could be played through an Akai synthesizer.

The brief for the image was quite tight – there had to be a girl, three acrobats and clapping hands – but the overall look was left to the artist.

The individual elements were assembled and photo-copied in black and white. The acrobats were based on figures taken from a book on yoga, and the leopard skin leotards – specified by the agency – were shapes cut from photocopies of leopards taken from a book on wild animals. The whole picture was assembled and copied on a colour copier, and parts of the image were coloured. The blue stripes of the background were created using blue paper with the copying process varying the edges and tone. It was only at this stage that photographs of the actual products were added, since they had to have a sharp, high-quality appearance.

Esso

The advertising agency supplied a visual which showed a horseshoe magnet, complete with the Esso tiger stripes, the idea being to attract young people into the company. The artist wanted to stress the magnetic pull – in the original visual the figures seemed to be merely strolling toward the magnet – and to do this he accentuated the perspective and enlarged the crowd.

It is worth noting that these amendments were agreed in conversations with the advertising agency. Such work is seldom a matter of unrestrained flights of fancy on the part of the artist; the advertising agencies have spent time and money researching and creating the initial image and would not thank an illustrator for turning their idea upside down.

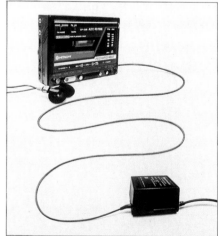

Above Chris Moore (A. P.) *Hitachi:* airbrush, 24 × 30 in (61 × 76 cm)

Left Simon Edwards *Akai:* photo collage, 11 × 16½ in (29 × 42 cm)

Left Chris Riddell (A. P.) *Esso:* pen and ink, 8 × 8 in (20 × 20 cm)

Pool Table

The client wanted a photographic image. They had several photographs of the pool table, but these did not fit in with the layout of the text, so the artist had to invent a precise three-point perspective image of the object to meet this requirement.

The first thing he did was to create a perspective grid which conformed to the space available, using his sound understanding of goemetry. The details of the table, extracted from the photographs, were transferred to the grid, and in this way the inadequate photographic reference was manipulated to create the desired effect.

The setting-out drawing was transferred to cartridge (drawing) paper and an airbrush used to establish the broad areas of colour. The wood finish and the chrome work were defined with a brush.

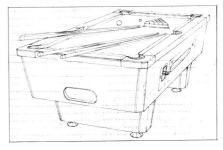

Left and above Bill Gregory (A. P.) *Pool Table:* airbrush, 11½ × 16½ in (29 × 42 cm)

Right Chris Moore (A. P.) *Monterez:* airbrush, 18 × 20 in (46 × 51 cm)

Far right Chris Moore (A. P.) *Looks Like a Winner:* airbrush, 17 × 17 in (43 × 43 cm)

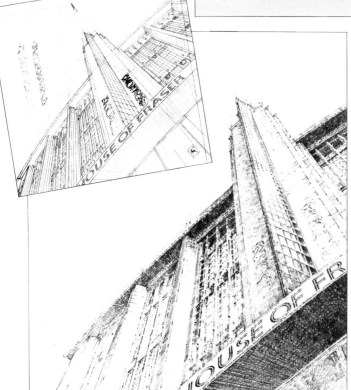

Above Bill Gregory (A. P.) *House of Fraser:* pencil, 16½ × 23 in (42 × 58.5 cm)

Monterez

This is an example of an illustration for which the airbrush artist is called in to achieve the kind of super-realism demanded by the art director's idea. This realism cannot be achieved by a camera; it had proved difficult to light the slightly opaque glass for photography and at the same time maintain the colour of the printed lettering. This airbrush artist was able to render both the quality of the glass and, with skilfull masking, the accuracy of the lettering.

House of Fraser

The art director wanted the artist to produce a loose version of his sketched visual that conformed precisely to the area available around the text.

A loose version in this case meant first establishing a drawing that was convincing architecturally and correct in perspective; to this end the artist was supplied with photographic reference. This drawing was projected using an epidiascope and then drawn in a freer manner with a soft pencil, a 4B.

The artist delivered the work to the client only to discover that alterations had been made to the building. He was supplied with a new set of photographs, and sat in the client's office armed with an eraser and pencils to make the necessary adjustments.

Above left and right Clare Hemstock (S.) *Swan Hellenic:* wood engraving, 1½ × 1 in (4 × 2.5 cm)

Below Clare Hemstock (S.) *Gloucester Docks Trading Co.:* wood engraving, 3½ × 3 in (9 × 7.5 cm)

Looks Like A Winner

Gloucester Docks Trading Co.

The artist was supplied by the client with a photograph of the rally car. However, he had to liaise closely with a photographer to obtain a photograph of the foreground car that conformed to the angle of the "reflected" image.

The rally car had been photographed with a telephoto lens while cornering at speed, and the wheels appeared distorted on the resulting photograph; it was the artist's job to make it look like a showroom model. The foreground car was amended slightly, (the aerial disappeared, for example, and was given a crisp reality) by the use of airbrush and brush-applied paint for the details.

Swan Hellenic

The artist was provided with photographic reference and an indication of the area to be filled by her two images: the request was for strong, but quite small images that would reproduce well on newsprint for a national newspaper.

Working "same size", the artist drew an indication of the shape on the block. The pavilion was a description of the form and line; but for the bird of paradise the colours of the photograph were converted into tonal "colours".

The client, requiring a logo for use on posters, letterheads, and general stationery, supplied the artist with a drawing which indicated the general layout – a reference to the docks and a ship in movement, preferably in sail. The client also indicated where the band of type was to run around the image.

The artist supplied a rough drawing of the image, received approval for it, and then set about drawing the block. The outline of the design was carefully established and the details traced down from the rough onto the block and reinforced with fountain-pen ink.

For the logo the image had to be reduced, but this caused the fine marks of the engraving to be lost, with the black filling in the white areas. A PMT reduction was made of the original, and black ink and white paint were used to re-establish the engraved quality, although with slightly heavier marks.

The combination of subject and technique has created a period look, ideally suited to this job.

The job was for a medical brochure, and the artwork was also to be used for presentation prints for mounting and framing as a wall display.

Such a re-creation of period, particularly when in a specifically scientific context, requires a great deal of research, and accordingly models were hired, dressed in the correct period costume, and photographed for reference. The artist had drawn a preparatory indication of the final image, and the figures were posed to conform to this, great care being taken with the studio lighting so that it gave the effect required for the finished artwork.

The artist used a smooth watercolour paper – the work was to be scanned – and since he wanted to convey a "period" look, he tinted the paper with pale sepia washes to give an appearance of ageing.

The image was drawn with an F pencil; the tones produced by the overlaying of marks and intense reworking in the dark areas.

Below Stuart Bodek (A. P.) *Laughing Gas:* pencil, 10 × 17 in (25.5 × 43 cm)

This is one page of a brochure, the aim of which was to indicate what happened in the six departments of this company. The artist chose to focus on one aspect of the activity rather than the physical environment or a descriptive illustration; and he took his own photographs for reference.

The editing panel, when photographed at a close, low angle, took on the appearance of a futuristic city. The airbrush techniques were skilfully employed to create this "double-take" – the glowing light, for example, is an effect ideally suited to the medium.

Left Chris Moore (A. P.) *Complete Video:* airbrush, 15 × 20 in (38 × 51 cm)

Top and above Bill Gregory (A. P.) *House of Lazard:* gouache, 4 × 12 in (10 × 30.5 cm)

The client wanted the clarity and air of sophistication that a painted illustration could give. A photograph of the image would have been difficult; as some of the objects – the key ring, for example – would have needed to be specially manufactured. In the painting, the artist created them himself as well as inventing the lighting effect, which would also have presented problems in a photographic set-up.

The artist was given a layout which indicated the area to be occupied by text, and he then established a convincing perspective arrangement of the assorted objects which fitted into the available space. Gouache was the medium chosen for the main part of the painting, but wherever a particularly brilliant colour was required, such as on the enamel on the top coin, ink was used. The shadows were stippled brushwork.

Quaife

A small photograph was supplied of the modern lorry, and this was projected using an epidiascope and the details searched out with a magnifying glass. A grid was drawn over the photocopy of the lettering which had been supplied by the client; the shapes were then transferred to the corresponding places on a grid drawn in perspective on the side of the lorry.

For the old van, the artist was supplied with a model, together with photographic reference for the house in the background; in the illustration the van had to conform to the same perspective as the house. A box was drawn in the proportions of the van, a grid put on each elevation and the details carefully located.

Above Bill Gregory (A. P.) *Quaife:* watercolour, 6¼ × 7½ in (16 × 19 cm) and 7½ × 7½ in (19 × 19 cm) Detailed pencil drawings were completed prior to the final artwork.

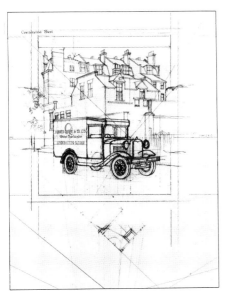

POSTERS

The Photon Connection

The client had presented a visual showing the development of hand-sets since the invention of the telephone. The artist did not find this a particularly eloquent image for a poster advertising a lecture on the use of fibre optics and infrared light in modern telecommunications. He thus created a striking poster which not only utilized the range of airbrush techniques to convey solid shape and glowing light, but also exploited the imagery often associated with air brush – futuristic technology. The eye is drawn to the sharply focused earpiece past the out-of-focus mouth piece as if looking along the side of a giant space ship.

Above Chris Moore (A. P.) *The Photon Connection:* airbrush, 15 × 21 in (38 × 30.5 cm)

Printer's Nightmare

The brief was to show a printing press rejecting the new paper developed by the advertiser, and it was to be shown in a Norman Rockwell manner. The brief was verbal rather than a closely defined plan.

The artist was required to submit a photocopy of the complete preparatory pencil drawing which was to form the basis of the painting. This allowed the client to be sure of the final image and, of course, to ask for alterations if necessary. Such an arrangement avoids the possible problem for the illustrator of having to completely re-paint an area that does not meet with the client's approval, since it is much easier to re-work a pencil drawing than a painting.

With an image in his mind of the total illustration the artist shot all the reference on black and white film.

Right Stuart Bodek (A. P.) *Printer's Nightmare:* acrylic, 20 × 28 in (51 × 71 cm)

Every element of the piece was recorded on film in accordance with the old adage of all realistic illustrators: "The final result is only as good as the reference". The more precise the photograph, in detail and lighting, the less adjustment has to be made by the artist. Stuart Bodek enjoys the benefit of a studio where, by the arrangement of specially fitted flood lights, the whole

range of natural and artificial light effects can be created.

Using an overhead epidiascope, which enabled him to work directly on the board, the artist projected down the many photographic images and experimented with their positioning. Eventually a final composition, in pencil outline, was achieved and approved, after which the painting was executed using acrylic paints.

Left and right (detail) Jane Mitchell (S.) *Tiger Letters:* gouache, 5 × 3¾ in (13 × 9.5 cm)

"Tiger" Letters

A set of posters 16 × 23" (40 × 58cm) was manufactured from the small gouache paintings, in which the colours were put down in a rapid and free manner to create a variety of texture and hue. In some places the paint was worked wet into wet; in others it was washed over a dried layer. The outline was drawn with chinagraph pencil.

The image was then enlarged by about five times, and the magnification created a number of interesting effects. The grain of the chinagraph pencil became a positive feature, and the black of the original mark dissolved into a range of browns and purples. The gradations and varied textures of the paint and the effect of the paint on the pencil took on more emphasis and thus increased the visual interest.

Theatre Group

In this example the artist had complete control from start to finish. The linocut image was printed on Japanese paper, cut out and pasted down onto the artwork sheet. The Hogarth-type speech bubbles were written with a technical pen, cut out and added to the image; and the instant lettering was also pasted on. The camera-ready artwork was a kind of collage – a single sheet covered with different types and shapes of paper.

Below Jane Smith *Theatre Group:* linocut, 16½ × 11¾ in (42 × 30 cm)

PACKAGING

This is an area in which the illustrator is seen as an artisan supplying a skill, a distinctive way of visualizing an art director's image, often within very precise limits. The type of package can vary enormously in shape and size, and the illustrations required can range from flat images to be viewed from one angle to images which cover the three dimensions of the object.

Soup Labels

This was a heavily directed piece of work, and the artist was supplied with a complete layout, with instructions on the area to be left free for type. The brief was to illustrate more than the product itself, and the finished artwork presents healthy ingredients set in a rural environment. The main colour of the label was provided so that the artist could choose colours for her illustration that worked with the surrounding area.

Above Biz Hull (A. P.) *Soup Labels:* coloured pencil

Sauce Labels

The image that the artist was asked to produce in this case was not that of the product but its place of origin. All the references for the view were provided by the design company with instructions to fade out the colour intensity in the area that was to bear the printed description.

Tea Packaging

The artist was given a lot of reference for this – copies of the advertising agency's mock-ups, photographs of the cup design and examples of specific colours which had to be matched accurately.

A completed image was sent for the client's approval, and it was felt that adjustments were needed, which were indicated on an annotated photocopy. It is the

nature of the pencil medium that colour mixing is not as easy as it is with paint, and in this case six different reds were used to achieve the required hue.

Although the artist was given samples of the tea to brew as instructed, it was difficult to indicate the difference between the two types, since there was no noticeable variation in colour. The smoothness of the liquid was also difficult to render – the criticism was made that it looked "hairy". Finally, the artist rubbed the surface gently with an eraser, to modify the colour without actually removing it, and then patiently built up layers of different coloured pencil to a smooth finish.

Wine Box

The box had already been designed, and so dictated to some extent the nature of the artwork. The front had a narrow dividing upright, which posed a problem. The

Top and above Biz Hull (A. P.) *Sauce Labels:* coloured pencil

Far left and left Biz Hull (A. P.) *Tea Packaging:* coloured pencil

Above Layout of the complete packaging design for the wine box.

Above left Pencil sketch for rear panel of the wine box (see **below left**) The artist, Bill Gregory (A. P.) used pen and ink for the final version.

Left This wine box incorporates the same rear and side design features (see **far left**), but a double arch was used for the front elevation to display the wines.

client wanted to create an impression of antiquity; and the artist was given some reference in the form of wine catalogues, and the image decided on was that of a wine cellar. To obtain an impression of solidity the dividing piece of cardboard was treated as a support viewed square on, while the flanking supports were allowed to show their sides in perspective.

The client also wanted an image of a lively drinking party with an 18th-century look. The artist found a 19th-century engraving which had the right kind of format, and used book reference to dress the characters in the correct period costume, embellishing the image with details of his own invention.

A technical pen was used for the drawing, and a sense of distance created by broken lines made of dots.

Tea Caddy

The artist was given a tin and had to construct her own template from observation and measurement. This was for the continuous elevation of the sides and the plan of the roof, complete with area for the hinge. A complication was presented by the procedure of printing the lid on a flat piece of tin, which was then stamped into the required shape – obviously the image would distort on the angles.

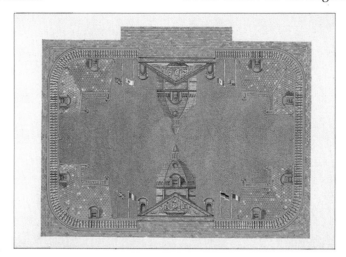

Right Susan Robertson (S.), design for the lid and side elevations of a tea caddy **below right**: gouache

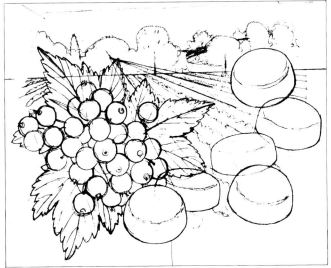

The client wanted a view of Harrods in the 1920s, complete with two vans and figures, so the artist researched the subject and took photographs of the building. The roughs were approved and the painting begun with gouache on stretched cartridge (drawing) paper, the main shapes being established in flat mid-tones and the forms and patterns worked up using darker and lighter tones. The sky was created with layers of colour stippled over a base tone and then blended with water.

Two alterations were asked for at this stage. In the original artwork the boy holding the balloon was feeding a horse drawing a Harrods' van, but it was now felt that the van should be changed to a motorized vehicle, so a careful repainting of the offending area had to be done. The second alteration was a minor one, simply the task of making the windows more blue.

Sweet Wrapper

The artist was given a tracing of the area available to him for his illustration and the visual requirements, in this case blackcurrants, foliage and the product itself. He produced an accurate pencil drawing for the client to approve or amend.

The requirement was to create a sort of heightened realism with intense colour and clear contrasts – too many fussy tones would not have printed and would generally confuse the image. The artist was also supplied with a Pantone colour reference for the packet so he could ensure that the colours used in the illustration would "read" clearly.

Fertilizer Bag

The artist based his pencil visualization on a rough supplied by the client. The vegetable grouping was approved as can be seen in the finished product.

Top left Stephen Adams (A. P.), pencil sketch for sweet wrapper **above right**

Above Stephen Adams (A. P.), pencil sketch for fertilizer bag **left**

TECHNICAL

Good technical illustration can stimulate the person leafing through a book to consult the text, sometimes even acting as a magnet for a subject which might not at first appear interesting. Having engaged the interest of the viewer, the ultimate aim is to convey a complete view of a subject, either by a collection of varied images or by one comprehensive statement.

Virgo Voyager

The research for this piece involved obtaining both photographs and technical information for such details as the hull lines. Preliminary sketches were made to establish angles and clarity, ensuring that the surface details of the boat did not get tangled up with the internal details in the ghosted illustration.

A perspective box was drawn on tracing paper, and the hull lines were plotted on it to establish the shape accurately. There was insufficient information to allow an accurate plotting of the interior, so several attempts and re-adjustments were made before it could be fitted into the drawing with convincing reality. All this was copied onto the master drawing, and final adjustments were made.

In order to preserve the state of the illustration board the image was "pushed through" onto the mask film using graphite paper. The background was sprayed first, which allowed the subsequent tones of the yacht to be related to the dark area, thus ensuring a visual

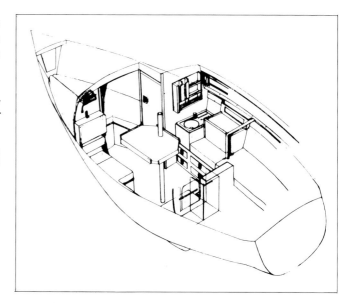

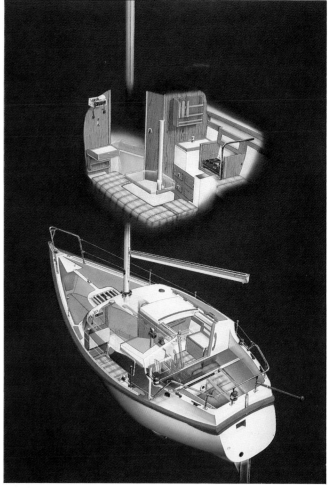

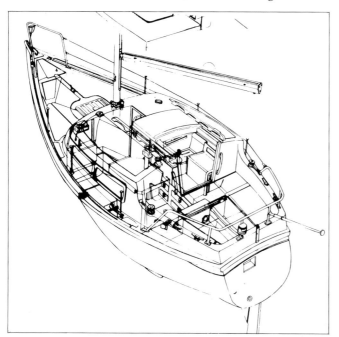

Above Jonathan Potter (S.) *Virgo Voyager:* airbrush, 20 × 13 in (51 × 33 cm)
Right Jonathan Potter (S.) *Harp:* airbrush, 23½ × 16¼ in (59.5 × 41 cm)

unity. Opaque paint was used for this. Masks were cut for different areas of the yacht and sprayed. In order to save time, much of the fine detail was painted in with watercolour, using a relatively dry brush. Brush-drawn lines were used throughout as outlines to lift areas away from the background, and opaque white was used for the highlights. To describe the chromium, the shapes were sprayed flat, the centre lightened with an eraser, and the highlights scratched in. Careful use of an eraser also produced the creases in the mattress.

Harp

The manufacturer supplied some diagrams of the construction, and the artist supplemented these with photographs taken from every conceivable angle.

The roughs were drawn and re-drawn in order to establish an exploded image that made visual sense. A prepared grid was used to ensure the accuracy of the final tracing, which was then transferred to a fine-surfaced paper.

The colour of the wood was sprayed down, the grain drawn in with a dryish brush along a straightedge and then re-sprayed to soften the harsh lines. The machine lines on the metal plates were scratched into a sprayed area and then re-sprayed; the process was repeated until the desired effect had been achieved. The gold area was sprayed, and an eraser then used to produce the highlights. The gold inlays were created by working a wet brush into a sprayed area.

The technical illustrator is able to produce images that give the viewer considerably more information and detail than a photograph could, and a greater indication of material and surface than a diagram.

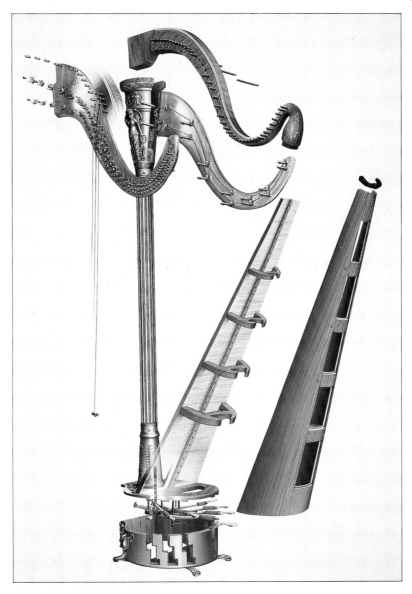

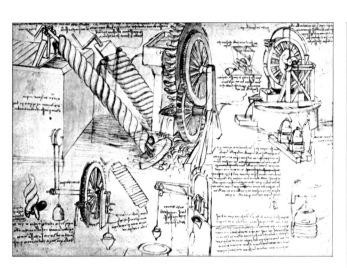

Above Leonardo da Vinci *Technical sketch* These drawings detail clearly and precisely the mechanics of Archimedes screws and water wheels.

Left Albrecht Dürer *Young hare* This very detailed study in watercolour reveals Dürer's precise observation of natural form.

Left This architectural sketch, attributed to Sir Christopher Wren, gives precise details of the plan, the exterior and, using a cut-away section, the interior of a dome.

Above Jane Reynolds (S.) *Shaggy ink caps:* watercolour, 7½ × 11 in (19 × 28 cm)

Shaggy Ink Caps

The most crucial aspect of technical, or botanical illustration in this case, is accurately recorded information. In preparation for this image the artist made drawings in the field – literally – and then took specimens back to her studio for further detailed drawings. In the case of the fungi speed was essential, since they die as quickly as they grow. The drawings charted different stages of growth and investigated different angles of view. Dissection in order to analyse the structure of an object is often a part of the early stages of image-making.

The sketches were made with an HB pencil with watercolour washed over. The emphasis is on accuracy; there is no room for artistic licence in this kind of work.

The final image was assembled and drawn on a thin watercolour paper stretched on a board. The colour was applied in tight washes and detail added with a drier brush; all the lines were reinforced with watercolour in case the pencil marks were lost in the printing process. Accurate colour matching was essential throughout ·

Penguins

The information gathering in this case was done "on site", and took the form of a great many drawings capturing both the broad appearance of the subject and the slight nuances and subtleties. Photographs rarely achieve the accuracy of detail which is essential for this type of illustration. The artist, however, can indicate subtle changes of form, which are often flattened in photography, by drawing or painting a series of "life" sketches.

Such drawings are frequently only indications of particular aspects of the subject matter, just as the colour notes, made in watercolour, are rarely complete – animate objects do have a tendency to move. Written descriptions of form, colour and even the character of the animal were used to supplement the sketches. It does not matter how obscure such jottings are; as long as they mean something to the illustrator they are invaluable as *aides-mémoire*. Often a lot of time is spent just observing the subject before its essential qualities become apparent.

The illustration had to describe the zoo environment of the penguins while concentrating on the birds themselves. Consequently, the penguins, in their many characteristic attitudes, were painted in great detail while the background was dealt with in a more summary fashion, ignoring any details such as cracked or stained concrete. In this way a visual separation was achieved, with the penguins given primary importance.

Left and above Jane Reynolds (S.) *Penguins:* watercolour, 8 × 11 in (20 × 28 cm)

Shopping Precinct

In this view of an imaginary precinct the artist was able to impose an ideal perspective scheme. The position of the horizon and hence the establishment of vanishing points was up to the artist, who did not have the constriction of relating the image to a real place.

Right Bill Gregory (A. P.) *Sketch of a shopping precinct:* pen and ink, 11½ × 16½ in (29 × 42 cm)

Hotel

The view required by the client was beyond the capacity of a camera to reproduce without distortion , as the angle of view was too wide. It was the artist's job to make an attractive image of a view from one side of a "well" created by the tall buildings and to put into this image the detail which the human eye might take in when surveying the whole.

Right Bill Gregory (A. P.) *Hotel:* watercolour and airbrush, 18 × 18 in (46 × 46 cm) The architectural detail was culled from photographic reference **below** to produce the accurate pencil drawing **inset right** on which the final artwork was based.

At the time of the commission, the buildings were in the process of being redeveloped and cleaned; they were partially covered with scaffolding and the fountain had not been put into place. The artist took photographs of the different elements which were to make up the image. These photographs, when montaged together, were to be the essential basis of his "setting-out" drawing, as he had been given plans but no architectural drawings of the elevations. The artist was confronted with two problems. The first involved patiently sorting out the architectural detail from the photographs, and the second, which demanded an intelligent, methodical imagination, was the establishment of a geometrically convincing layout which worked as an attractive image. To complicate matters, the courtyard was not square, and thus the two walls that formed the sides of the well did not share a common vanishing point.

Paying strict attention to the rules of two-point perspective the artist produced a reconstruction of the architectural environment, mapping out the three-dimensional reality on the flat plane of the paper. For this technically-exact drawing hard pencils – 3H and 6H – were used. These permitted mathematical precision in the arrangements of line and did not smudge as the artist's hand moved across the paper.

A photocopy of the drawing was sent to the client for approval, and then the image was put on a lightbox and traced through onto the cartridge (drawing) paper which was to take the final painting. The buildings were masked out, and the sky was sprayed on using an airbrush. The architecture was painted in watercolour washes, using hues which gave a fresh quality to the surfaces.

BOOK COVERS

Generally, illustrations for book covers are designed to indicate the content matter and to catch the eye, while leaving something to the imagination of the potential reader.

When the Lion Feeds

The client wanted a montage type of image, in the style of cinema posters.

The artist searched out book reference for the animals and gun, while he himself photographed models for the human elements. All this assembled, the image was traced through onto a board and the image painted using a fine acrylic technique.

Musicians of Auschwitz

The artist was asked to portray three women with their instruments. She read the book, shot the photographic reference and produced three roughs, after which a small portable epidiascope was used to project the photographs onto the paper so that the image could be arranged in terms of outline.

The mood of the book was expressed by the use of grey paper, which set the predominant colour of the piece. The way in which the pastel was used also added to the mood; it is not an elegant blending of shades but a stark, striking use of the side of the pastel, particularly effective in the faces.

Above Kevin Tweddell (A. P.) *When the Lion Feeds:* acrylic, 19½ × 12 in (49.5 × 30.5 cm)

Above Debbie Hinks (A. P.) *Musicians of Auschwitz:* pastel, 24 × 22 in (61 × 56 cm)

Horrocks

The artist was supplied with three separate photographs from which to make this portrait: one had the required facial expression, one had the correct uniform, and one the correct hat. The three images were brought together using an epidiascope, their size adjusted and a complete drawing made.

The variety of reference brought with it attendant problems. The required face was hatless, so the artist had to create the effect of the cast shadow. All the shots were Second World War black and whites, so the detail had to be worked up more or less from scratch, and the ribbons and decorations had to be accurately researched for the correct colours.

The clients wanted an "oil portrait" type of image, and to produce this the artist used a canvas board primed with emulsion paint, employing a loose, painterly acrylic technique.

Bunuel

It was not easy to find photographic reference of the film director Luis Buñuel as an older man, and in the end the artist had to use a photographic library, from which she hired a suitable photograph.

The clients also wanted to see memorable images from the subject's films featured on the cover, so the artist created a shape from torn coloured paper and drew the images on it. The final piece contained a range of different pastel marks, from the smooth construction of the face to the texture of the fur collar.

The first, blue, version was rejected by the clients, and so a second was executed in accordance with their preferences.

D. H. Lawrence

The brief was for a portrait which was not just a likeness but a positive indicator of character. The artist submitted three different pencil drawings on layout paper as well as a colourvisual as an indication of the proposed colour treatment.

The selected image was drawn up and transferred to watercolour paper by means of a lightbox. An irregular quality was created around the face by laying down a wash, covering it with a water-soluble glue and then painting over the area, which washed away the glue in a random manner. The flesh, beard and hands were painted with straight acrylic heightened with charcoal. After experimenting with a variety of textures for the jacket, the artist achieved the desired quality with paper kitchen towel; the crumpled paper was painted and the different tones thus produced were stuck on.

The clients had approved the full-torso image, and the artist accordingly supplied this, though in the printed cover the figure was cropped.

Top Stuart Bodek (A. P.) *Horrocks:* acrylic, 17 × 12 in (43 × 30.5 cm)

Middle Debbie Hinks (A. P.) *Buñuel:* pastel, 20 × 13 in (51 × 33 cm)

Above right Colin Williams *D. H. Lawrence:* acrylic and collage, 25 × 20 in (63.5 × 51 cm) The artist first completed a visual **above left** as a guide to the proposed colour treatment.

Willow Street Kids

The brief asked for four children, whose characters were specified, complete with schoolbags, peering over a wall on which falls the shadow of a sinister stranger. Armed with the description of the children, the artist went to a local school where, with the assistance of the teaching staff, he shot photographic reference.

The visual was presented and the clients made various amendments, such as a re-arrangement of the children. Since the typography was to go on the wall area, the artist was asked to replace the red bricks with a cement surface. Once the image had been transferred to the painting surface the artist began with the parts of immediate interest to the viewer – the faces. The texture of the wall was created using a fine natural sponge loaded with very dilute watercolour.

Above right John Marriott (A. P.) *The Willow Street Kids:* watercolour, 17 × 11½ in (43 × 29 cm) The artist shot his own photographic reference **top left and right** and devised the initial figure grouping **above left**, which was revised for the finished artwork.

The Maul and the Pear Tree

The designer of this jacket planned to create a poster-like effect, requiring a pictorial image as part of the design. The illustrator was given an old print for reference and asked to render it in pen and ink with washes of watercolour to give an oldfashioned tinted appearance. He was instructed to work to set proportions so that the artwork could be reduced down to fit the intended area of the design. He was also asked to rearrange elements of the original print to make the image clearer, and figures were removed from the foreground and composed into a crowd, leaving the central image clear and uncluttered. The hole in which the body was to be buried was more strongly defined, and one of the background buildings was transformed by the addition of a sign into the public house of the title.

Beginner's Love

This book image was for one of a series of books aimed at the teenage market, and the artist was instructed to break away from the customary images and to exploit those suggested by the text. He read the book, discussed his ideas with the art director and hired professional models for photography. He then produced a pencil rough – an outline drawing with details of the facial expression and an indication of the general tones – executed with a 3B pencil. The comparative softness of the pencil allowed a speedy but positive indication of the image.

The original design showed the girl in the process of removing her T-shirt, but although this was an appropriate image, the publishers thought it likely to offend, and consequently it was changed to a "provocative" pose, which necessitated new photographs of the model.

Below Chris Riddell (A. P.) *The Maul and the Pear Tree:* pen and ink

Below Stuart Bodek (A. P.) *Beginner's Love:* acrylic, 11 × 11 in (28 × 28 cm)

Right Stephen Adams (A. P.) *A Cat in the Window:* gouache, 14 × 18 in (35.5 × 45.5 cm)

A Cat in the Window

For this book, one of a series featuring the author's life with his pet animals, the artist met the author and took photographic reference at his home.

The top third of the format had to be kept clear for type, with the spine left relatively free, and a space left on the back for information. Accordingly, the artist allowed the image to flow across the available space while ensuring that the front had a strong visual presence of its own. The wall was rendered in a loose, thin gouache and kept pale to enable the typography to show up well. The lower part of the front image was painted in a much tighter manner with much greater intensity of colour. On the back, the sky presented a clear area for the type.

One Winter of the Holy Spirit

This book cover demonstrates the adaptability of the good illustrator. Because of pressure of time the artist was asked to produce a front cover only, but later the client changed his mind and asked for a wrap-around. There was insufficient time for the realization of a completely new cover, so the artist conceived the spine and back as "add-ons". When the book was published in paperback form she was asked to heighten the colour of the front, since that alone would be printed. This explains the difference in our illustration.

Left Biz Hull (A. P.) *One Winter of the Holy Spirit:* coloured pencil, 12 × 17 in (30.5 × 43 cm)

CHILDREN'S BOOKS

Humphrey's New Trousers

This book was about a single character, so the illustrator had to be able to maintain a consistent characterization from all angles and in all circumstances. The images here are part of the narrative of the book, with each one telling a story, rather than spotlighting individual moments.

Colour in this case was used to form shapes and to indicate rather than to describe.

The Stone-Headed Giant

The story line in this traditional fairy-tale book was strong and detailed. The artist was obliged to seize a significant incident and illustrate it with attention to the text but also with an eye to embellishing the picture with extra detail.

The drawing was tight, with the textural variation and tonal changes described by using the full range of pen marks. The fully developed drawing then received colour, which was used to describe the surface qualities and to suggest the spatial recession.

Left Chris Riddell (A. P.) *The Stone-Headed Giant:* pen and ink, 8 × 5¾ in (20 × 14.5 cm)

Top and above Chris Riddell (A. P.) *Humphrey's New Trousers:* pen and ink, 7½ × 6½ in (19 × 16.5 cm)

Noisy Poems

The editor wanted to see a mock-up of the book, which was to include accurate guides to the finished images and two pieces of finished artwork indicating the technique to be used. This arrangement allowed the editor to study the project and suggest alterations before the complete artwork had been produced. The original plan, in which the poems appeared inside voice bubbles, was rejected.

The colour rough reveals the artist's experiments with subject, form and colour. Undecided on how to portray the ground, he drew a paved surface to the left of the illustration and a muddy field to the right. Two arm positions were also indicated and the raised adjustment was eventually chosen to create a livelier expression.

Millie Mouse

The designer presented the artist with an idea for a book for young children featuring one of the artist's favourite characters. Supplied with the words, she created suitable images directly with the brush using gouache paint.

The format of the book presented a number of problems – in particular the cut-out windows and the consequent precision required in the placing of the figures; this demanded a close working relationship between designer and artist.

Far left Nick Sharratt *Noisy Poems:* crayon, 18½ × 21 in (47 × 53 cm) A rough sketch **above left** was translated into a colour visual **above right** for client approval.

Left *Millie Mouse* Artwork by Annette Alcock (D. W. D.): gouache

GREETING CARDS

 The variety of greeting cards is vast; they bear messages for all occasions and images for all tastes. Here we see three variations on the Christmas-card theme.

Robin in a Winter Landscape

This image incorporated some of the "required" elements of traditional Christmas card design – where there is a robin there must be snow, and the predominate colours must be red and green. In addition to adhering to these basics, the artist depicted a church in his customary accurate gouache technique.

Owls

In this image the artist explored the decorative possibilities of familiar, seasonal images. Pattern was used to the full in the feathers on the owls, the foliage of the trees and the fall of snow. The solid colour properties of gouache are ideal for this purpose.

Moorgate Card

The artist was asked to produce one of the several images planned for the numerous surfaces of a folded Christmas card. He was given a designer's sketch which he could develop in any way he liked – an open brief which had an element of fun.

After the basic design had been established, the preparatory drawing, which contained all the complicated details of the finished image, was carefully

constructed. All the problems of draughtmanship were solved at this stage, providing a black and white skeleton which could be transferred to the painting surface and then given the flesh of colour and texture.

All the print was hand painted and the mask cut for the airbrush stage; pink was sprayed over the page area, with brown and black used to create the shadows. Texture was produced using the splatter method in the background, and the plug and lead were established with an airbrush, with some adjustment made by hand – for example, the stippled highlight on the plug.

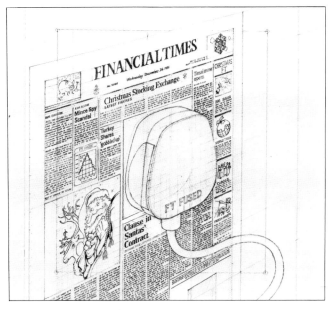

Far left Stephen Adams (A. P.) *Robin in a Winter Landscape:* gouache, 12 × 10 in (30.5 × 25.5 cm)
Left Annette Alcock (D. W. D.) *Owls:* gouache, 7 × 5 in (18 × 13 cm)

Left Bill Gregory (A. P.) *Moorgate card:* airbrush, 7 × 6¾ in (18 × 17 cm) The artist made numerous preparatory sketches **above left** before constructing a detailed pencil drawing **above right**.

CALENDAR

The brief was loose – a scroll-format calendar with countryside images which did not have to correspond to the particular month. The artist chose to combine images based on a particular village with details of plants.

A large number of sketches were made on location, and a rough layout was produced which indicated, in colour, the artist's intended scheme. The rough consisted of painted fragments assembled to fit the format; layout paper was used for this, since it allowed some transparency and therefore made the assembly easier.

The client made a number of observations which made it necessary for the artist to make alterations; the village had to be relegated to the distance, some buildings had to be eliminated, the format had to become a series of vignettes, and the road signs had to disappear since many of the calendars were to be sold abroad. A specific consideration was the distinct layout of the days of each month – for example a leaf could not be allowed to run into an area where it would obliterate the last day of the month.

The final artwork had to be presented in two pieces for the printing process, and consequently the artist made sure that the design had a natural break at the division point.

Right Jane Reynolds (S.) *Calendar:* watercolour, 19 × 9 in (48 × 23 cm) The artist based the final artwork on carefully observed sketches taken in the field **left**.

DESIGN STUDIO

DESIGN STUDIO

The design studio is the place where commercial projects – promotional and point-of-sale material and so on – are developed from start to finish. As we have seen on the previous pages artwork is often commissioned from illustrators working in specialist fields, but illustrations are also frequently executed by the studio itself.

The emphasis is usually on the immediately effective image which can be rapidly produced, and consequently the specially designed, time-saving products available to the designer are extensively used. One such product is the dry transfer sheet of tone.

Train

The drawing was established on smooth surfaced art-board and the sheet of tone laid over it; the required shape was cut around using a very sharp scalpel and the sheet was pulled away, leaving the area covered.

In this instance the dark tones were established first, which enabled the artist to cut out shapes where necessary. These shapes could then be given a different tone. Locating such a secondary tone had to be done with great care, firstly to avoid leaving a gap of white board between the shapes, and secondly to ensure that a third tone was not created by the overlapping of the two tones. Incisions in the board had to be avoided since they would be evident in reproduction.

The lines of dots within the sheet were lined up with those of the areas already laid down. The pieces of tone were initially firmed down with finger pressure, which allowed re-adjustments where necessary, and burnished down flat when the job was completed, providing a perfectly flat image for the printer.

Brands Hatch Morgan

The brief was to design a corporate image for use on stationery, car-stickers, T-shirts, etc, and a number of rough ideas were submitted to the client. He selected the one featuring a cartoon image.

For use as a press ad the image was prepared as black and white artwork. The image of the man and car was drawn using a technical pen, as was the chequered flag, and the lettering was done with instant lettering. The colours of the Union Jack were converted into tones.

The artwork was then sectioned into the colours in which it was to be printed. On the art-board a PMT of the area to be printed black was stuck down, and two overlays – one indicating the areas to be printed blue, the other those to be red – were located on the appropriate part of the image. A sheet of photo-opaque film was laid over the artwork and cut around the shape, care being taken to allow a bleed onto the black line. The negative area was then removed.

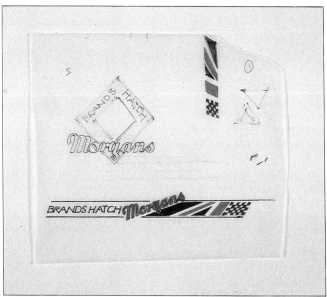

Far left Graham Farenden *Train:* instant tone

Bottom Peter Kay *Brands Hatch Morgan:* pen and ink, instant tone and lettering, 3 × 10 in (7.5 × 25.5 cm) Several sketches were made **left** before the basic design was established in black and white **below.**

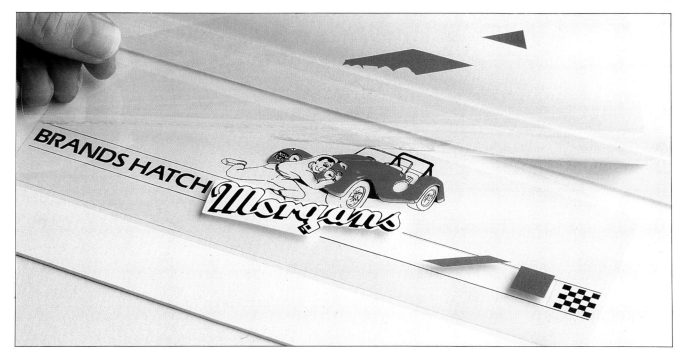

*A*PPENDIX

THE ILLUSTRATOR

Many illustrators I have spoken to are resigned to the fact that the public take the pictorial printed image for granted. I hope the preceding pages will have established that a great deal of thought and process go into producing the everyday commercial image.

So what is the nature of an illustrator's working life? It is, of course, as varied as the different types of image and commission; no two artists are alike, work alike, or are employed in the same way. The illustrator is a visual specialist who puts his or her talents to the service of a client or designer, but within this broad definition there is almost infinite variety, and some jobs demand slavish adherence to instructions while others allow considerable creative freedom.

The work itself can be irregular too, bringing frantic rushes of activity with long, unsociable hours, followed by quiet periods and a reduced income. It was surprising to find how many of the artists I interviewed were in the middle of a job commissioned on the Friday for delivery the following Monday. Many illustrators chose to work on their own in their own studio, which is often part of their home, and although this makes them masters of their lives, it does require a considerable self-discipline. Others prefer to work as part of a group, sharing resources and the expense of large items of equipment and enjoying the stimulus of the exchange of ideas.

Persuading potential clients to see examples of their work is obviously of vital importance to the illustrator. The two most direct methods are self-promotion and representation by an artists' agency. An agency has the advantage of having many contacts but they do, of course, take a commission for their services. Exhibitions and competitions are another way in which an illustrator's images and style can be kept in the commercial eye.

The portfolio is the artist's personal showcase. A collection of one type of work in a particular style can have a great impact, while a portfolio containing a variety of styles of work in different areas shows versatility. Often, of course, securing a job is a matter of the portfolio being in the right place at the right time.

Organization is a key word for the illustrator. Time has to be allowed for the various stages: researching a brief, assembling the image, receiving the client's approval, and then producing the finished artwork. Time is money, and methods and techniques in illustration often have to be viewed as problem solvers rather than being chosen for aesthetic reasons; for example, a particular paint may be chosen for its fast-drying properties. Personal experiment is the key not just to an individual style but also to the efficient production of artwork.

Adaptability is a desirable quality in the illustrator; an ability to compromise stylistic principles in order to comply with a client's demands. So is a thick skin; it is easy for an illustrator to feel offended when it is clear that he or she is being regarded as merely a resource in the impersonal world of commerce.

The illustrator also needs to be well organized in terms of communications. The telephone is the life-line, and equally important is a knowledge of all the methods of despatching roughs and artwork, such as those offered by the Post Office and, in some countries, the rail network. But perhaps the most crucial area of organization is money. Invoices must be carefully prepared, copies should be kept of all correspondence, and care should be taken to establish at the outset exactly what rights are being bought by the client. Artist agencies do take care of many of these aspects, but the artist is well advised to keep his or her own records.

ORGANIZATIONS

A very useful booklet entitled *The Illustrator's Survival Kit*, providing a great deal of information for illustrators, including financial matters, is published in Britain by The Association of Illustrators. Membership of this organization, provides, among other things, legal advice and a slide bank used by clients.

The Association of Illustrators
1 Colville Place
off Charlotte Street
London W1P 1HN.

The American body, the Society of Illustrators, was founded at the beginning of this century to "promote and stimulate interest in the art of illustration, past, present and future". The Society is deeply involved with educational projects, and has instituted the Student Scholarship Competition for college level art students. The Society opened the Museum of American Illustration in 1981 and also maintains the Library of American Illustration for research purposes.

The Society of Illustrators
128 East 63rd Street
New York, N.Y. 10021

The Canadian Association of Photographers and illustrators in Communications offers a wide selection of services to its members, including discount rates for travel, art and photographic supplies and an insurance package covering equipment and studio liability. The Association holds an annual show of selected work by its members, and is in the process of organizing a publication on "Business Practices and Guidelines".

CAPIC/ACPIP
275 King Street East
P.O. Box 186
Toronto, Ontario M5A 1K2

GLOSSARY

A

ACETATE Clear sheet used for overlaying images.

ALLA PRIMA A method in which the paint is worked directly in order to finish the image in one session.

ARTWORK The completed illustration sent to the printer for reproduction.

B

BITE The action of acid in the etching of a metal plate.

BLEED An extension of the image beyond the format.

BLEED-PROOF WHITE *see* Process white.

BRIEF The verbal or written instructions supplied by a client or art director upon which the artist bases his or her illustration.

BROMIDE A photographic print on a paper coated with silver bromide; loosely used for PMT.

C

COPY Written work to be printed on the page.

D

DRY-BRUSH A technique of fine pencil-like strokes made by a brush loaded with paint which is then squeezed to remove much of the liquid.

E

EPIDIASCOPE Optical device for projecting slides, photographs and, in some cases, three-dimensional objects.

F

FORMAT The required size and shape of an image.

G

GROUND The surface on which an image is painted.

H

HATCHING Parallel marks laid down to create tones or solidity of form.

I

IMPASTO Paint directly applied very thickly so that it retains the mark of paintbrush or knife.

L

LAYOUT A generalised sketch which indicates the position of the illustration on a printed page, showing the areas to be taken up by printed matter.

M

MASK Covering an area of an image in order to preserve its apperance during the application of another colour or during another part of the process.

MONTAGE The assembly of parts of photographs or drawings to make another image.

N

NEWSPRINT Unsized paper used for newspapers.

O

OVERLAY A transparent sheet bearing indications of extra colour or tones to be placed over the basic artwork.

P

PANTONE The trade name of one system of colour reference encompassing inks, pens and papers.

PHOTOCOPY An immediate copy of artwork, generally in black and white.

PMT Photo-mechanical transfer; a type of photographic print made on a very versatile copying machine; also called a velox.

PRIMER A coating on the support which acts as a ground for oil and acrylic painting.

PROCESS CAMERA A camera used for making negatives for block and plate making.

PROCESS WHITE Opaque white paint used for correcting an image.

PROOF A print made from a block, plate or screen in order to establish the state of the image during the process.

R

REFERENCE Specific source material. This may be specially photographed or researched from books, magazines and libraries. Illustrators often build up their own library of source images.

ROUGH A broad indication of the intended image.

S

SCANNER An electronic device for producing colour separations for printing.

SUPPORT The surface on which a painted image is made.

T

TORCHON Tightly rolled paper forming a point, used for fine blending of charcoal and pastel. Also known as tortillon or stump.

TOOTH Roughness of a support which enables the paint or other medium to grip the surface; also called key.

U

UNDERPAINTING The indication of tonal values or areas of colour as the first stage of a painting in oils or acrylic.

V

VISUALS Initial ideas of the possible image.

INDEX

A.P.

ARTIST PARTNERS LTD
14–18 Ham Yard
Great Windmill Street
London W1

S.W.

STARTWORKS
Studio 7A
75 Filmer Road
London SW6

D.W.D.

DEVAN-WETTON DESIGN
23 South Terrace
London SW7

PICTURE CREDITS

Key: *t* = top; *b* = bottom; *l* = left; *r* = right; *c* = centre.

The author and publishers have made every effort to identify the copyright owners of the photographs; they apologise for any omissions and would like to thank the following:

p.7 Trinity College, Dublin **p.8** Bridgeman Art Library **p.9** E.T. Archive **p.25** E.T. Archive **p.26** *l* British Museum **p.27** *tl* Colin Williams *tr* Colin Williams/art direction: Atyeo, Cork & Linklater *br* Nic Sharratt/*Exchange Contracts* **p.28** *t* Louvre (Snark) **p.29** *tl* Stuart Bodek *tr* Jane Mitchell *br* Biz Hull/Methuen, London **p.30** *l* Biz Hull/Sphere Books Ltd **p.30/31** Biz Hull/Methuen, London **p.31** *tr* Chris Riddell/Jonathan Cape Ltd **p.32** National Gallery, London **p.33** *t* E.T. Archive **p.34** Debbie Hinks **p.35** Nick Sharratt **p.36** *t* British Museum *b* Mansell Collection **p.37** *l* Bill Gregory/Methuen, London *r* Chris Riddell/Penguin Books **p.38** *t* David Watson *b* Nick Sharratt/*Cosmopolitan*/National Magazine Co Ltd **p.39** Kevin Tweddell **p.40** Jane Smith **p.41** The Courtauld Institute, London **p.44** Jackie Campbell **p.45** Jane Reynolds **p.46** Jackie Campbell **p.47** John Marriott **p.48** Annette Alcock/Davan-Whetton Design **p.49** *l* Stephen Adams *r* Jane Smith/*She*/National Magazine Co Ltd **p.50** *t* Susan Robertson *b* Stephen Adams/British Reader's Digest **p.51** The National Gallery, London **p.52** *r* Philip O'Reilly **p.53** University Art Gallery, Nabraska **p.55** Bill Gregory/Royle **p.57** courtesy Shoot that Tiger! **p.58/9** Kevin Cunningham **p.59** *r* Chris Moore **p.60** *t* Simon Edwards *b* Simon Edwards/*Time Out*/Art Dir. Simon Bishop **p.61** *t* Caroline Grimshaw *b* David Watson/first appeared in *New Scientist*, London, the weekly review of science and technology **p.63** Jonathan Potter **p.64** Chris Moore/ Art Dir. Gary Day-Ellison/Pan Books Ltd **p.65** *t* Chris Moore/ Methuen, London *b* Chris Moore/Octopus Books Ltd **p.68** E.T. Archive **p.69** Jane Smith **p.70** Jane Smith/*City Limits* **p.71** Jane Smith *tl* Jane Smith/David Davies Assoc for Midland Bank plc **p.72/73** E.T. Archive **p.74/75** Clare Hemstock **p.76** Victoria & Albert Museum, London **p.77** Victoria & Albert Museum **p.80** Caroline Grimshaw **p.81** *t* Caroline Grimshaw *bl br* Gino D'Achille/ from *As We Forgive* by Barbara Hale, pub. Corgi Books **p.82** coll. Mlle. Marcelle Lender **p.82/83** Kevin Cunningham **p.84/85** Jane Mitchell **p.85** *l* Caroline Grimshaw *r* Jane Mitchell **p.88** *l* Simon Edwards/*Car Magazine r* David Watson/*Here's Health* **p.89** *t* Susan Robertson/*Good Housekeeping*/National Magazine Co Ltd *b* Jane Smith/courtesy *Over 21* Magazine **p.90** Debbie Hinks/courtesy *Woman Magazine* **p.91** *t* Biz Hull/courtesy *Woman* Magazine *bl br* Debbie Hinks **p.92** *l* Simon Edwards/Ad. Agency: Hicks & Hayes Ltd for Akai's Electronic Musical Instruments *r* Chris Moore/Newton & Godin Agency for Hitachi Sales (UK) Ltd **p.93** *t* Chris Riddell/courtesy Esso UK plc *b* Bill Gregory/Option One **p.94** *t* Chris Moore/Blackburn's Packaging Design Consultants *b* Bill Gregory/Connel May & Stevenson for House of Fraser **p.94/95** Chris Moore/Newton & Godin Agency for Lancia UK **p.95** *t* Clare Hemstock/Yellowhammer for Swan Hellenic *b* Clare Hemstock/The Small Back Room for Pierce Developments Ltd **p.96** *l* Stuart Bodek *r* Bill Gregory/BdO Group for Lazard Brothers (Des. Barry Ozard/Creative Dir. John White) **p.97** Bill Gregory/ Islington Design Co Ltd for Quaife Paper Ltd **p.98** *l* Chris Moore/courtesy STC plc *r* Jane Mitchell *b* Stuart Bodek **p.99** *t* Jane Mitchell *b* Jane Smith/ Unfortunati Commedia Theatre Co **p.100** Biz Hull/Holmes & Marchant **p.101** *t* Biz Hull/Michael Peters & Partners Ltd for Oy Gustav Paulig AB (Finland) *b* Bill Gregory/ Marks & Spencer plc **p.102** Susan Robertson/Ian Logan Design Co **p.103** *t* Stephen Adams/Holmes & Marchant for Callard & Bowser Group *b* Stephen Adams/May & Baker Garden Care **p.104/105** Jonathan Potter **p.106** *t* Fotomas Index *c* Albertina, Vienna *b* RIBA, London **p.106/107** Jane Reynolds **p.108** *t* Bill Gregory **p.108/109** Bill Gregory/Maitland Hards Gill Advertising for St James Court Hotel p.110 *l* Kevin Tweddell/Art Dir. Gary Day-Ellison/Pan Books Ltd *r* Debbie Hinks/Sphere Books Ltd **p.111** *t* Stuart Bodek/Sphere Books Ltd *c* Debbie Hinks/Wm Collins Sons & Co Ltd *b* Colin Williams/J M Dent & Sons Ltd p.112 John Marriott/Art Dir. Gary Day-Ellison/Pan Books Ltd **p.113** *l* Chris Riddell/Sphere Books Ltd *r* Stuart Bodek/Art Dir. Gary Day-Ellison/Pan Books Ltd **p.114** *t* Stephen Adams/Sphere Books Ltd *b* Biz Hull/Macdonald & Co Ltd **p.114/115** Chris Riddell/Grafton Books (Collins Publishing Group) **p.115** Chris Riddell from *The Book of Giants*, published for J. Sainsbury plc by Walker Books Ltd (© 1985 Walker Books Ltd) **p.116** reproduced by permission of Oxford University Press from *Noisy Poems* collected by Jill Bennett, illustrated by Nick Sharratt. Illustrations © Nick Sharratt 1987. Selection, arrangement & editorial matter © Oxford University Press 1987 **p.117** Annette Alcock/Davan-Whetton Design for Methuen Children's Books **p.118** *l* Stephen Adams/Royle *c r* Annette Alcock/Davan-Whetton Design **p.119** Bill Gregory/Moorgate Group plc **p.120/121** Jane Reynolds/Popprint Products Ltd **p.122/123** Graham Farenden **p.123** Peter Kay/Brands Hatch Morgan.